AF413351

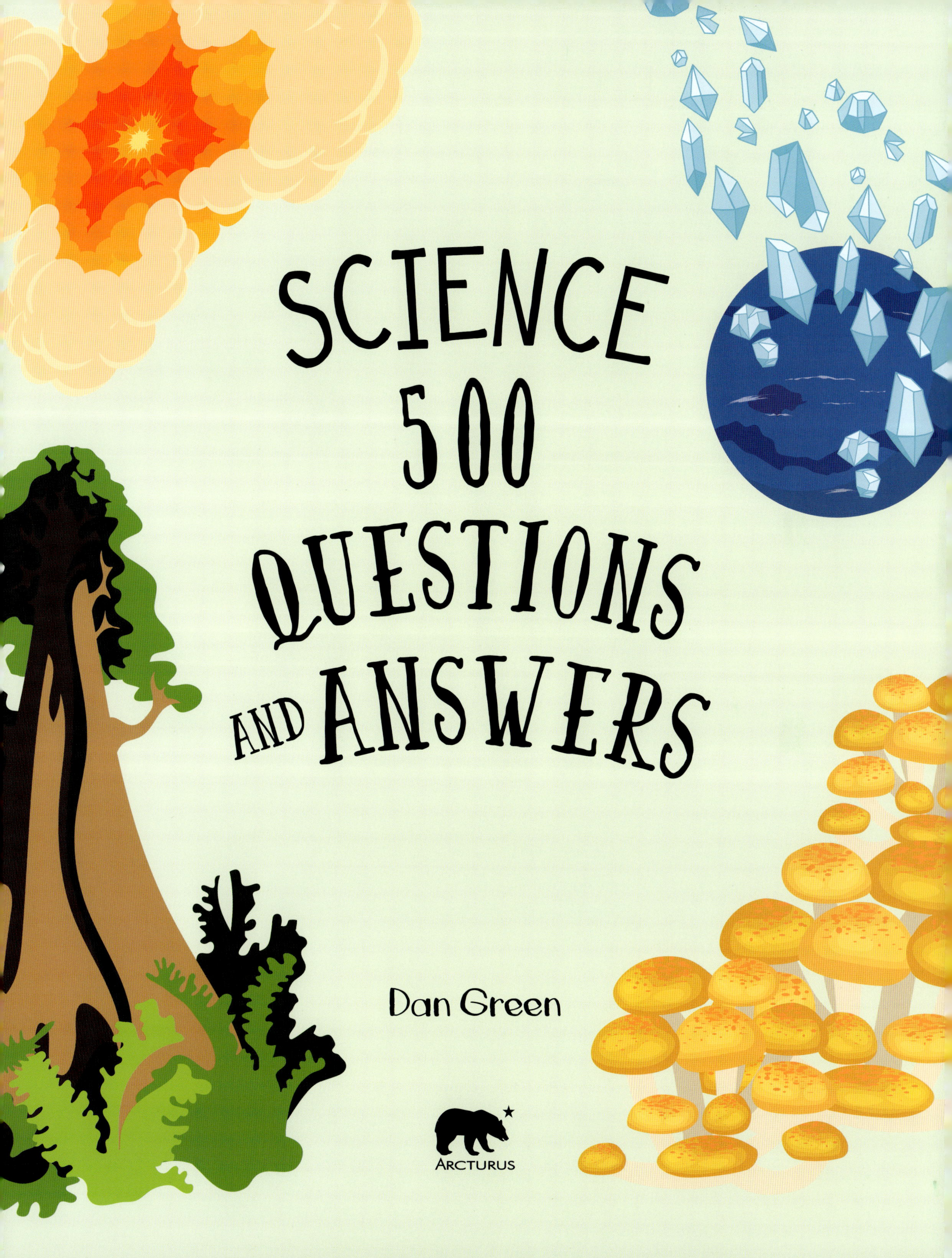

SCIENCE
500
QUESTIONS
AND ANSWERS
Dan Green
ARCTURUS

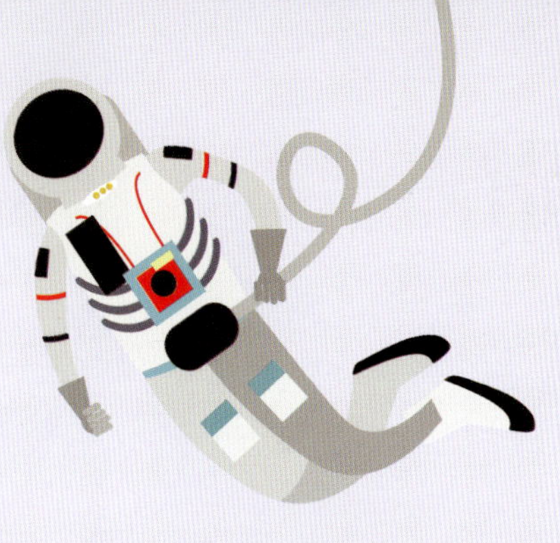

ARCTURUS

This edition published in 2026 by Arcturus Publishing Limited
26/27 Bickels Yard, 151–153 Bermondsey Street,
London SE1 3HA

Author: Dan Green
Illustrator: Jake McDonald
Editors: William Potter and Lydia Halliday
Designer: Sarah Fountain
Editorial Manager: Joe Harris
Managing Designer: Georgina Wood

ISBN: 978-1-3988-6866-3
CH012491US
Supplier 29, Date 0326, PI 00010556

Printed in China

INTRODUCTION

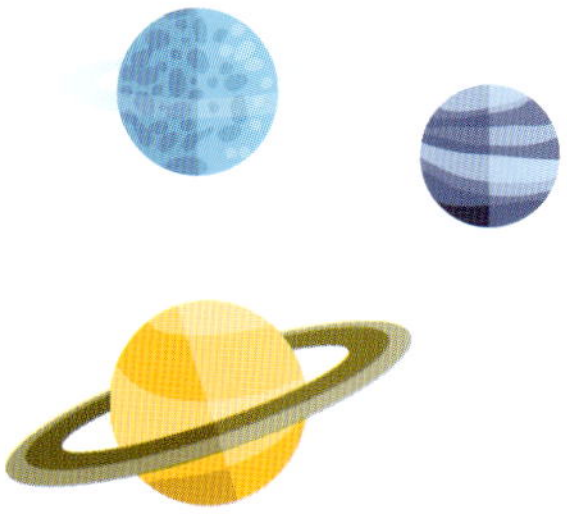

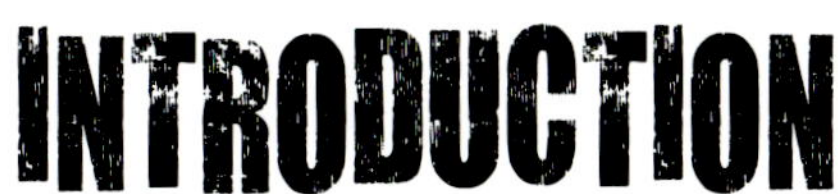

If you had a chance to ask a scientist any question, what would you ask?

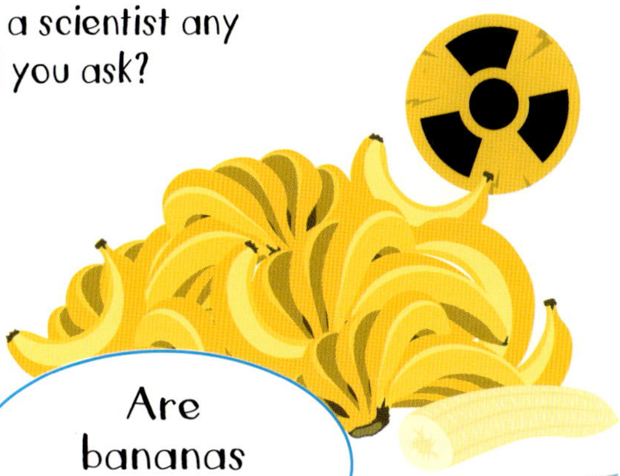

How heavy is your brain?

How old is the Solar System?

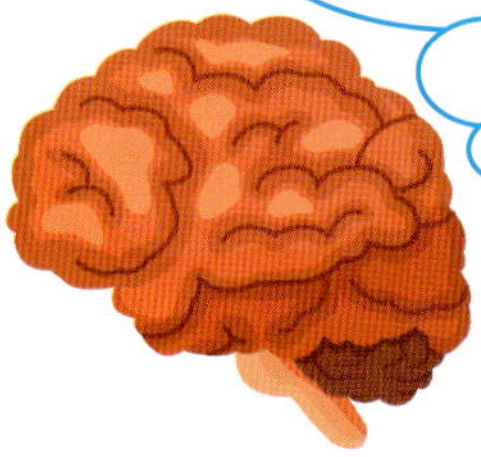

Are bananas radioactive?

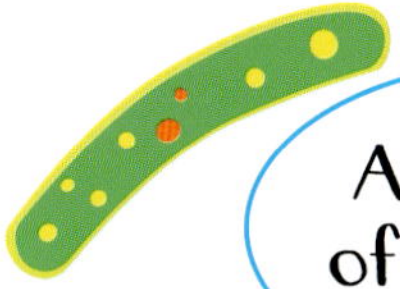

Are we full of bacteria?

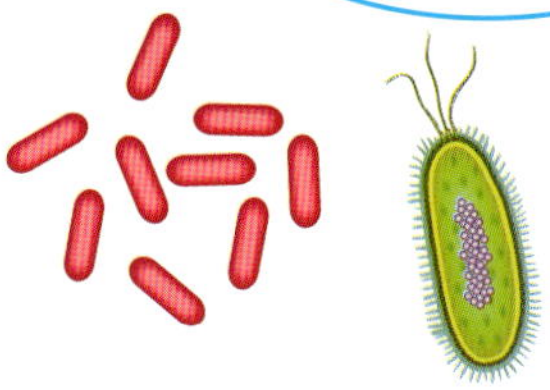

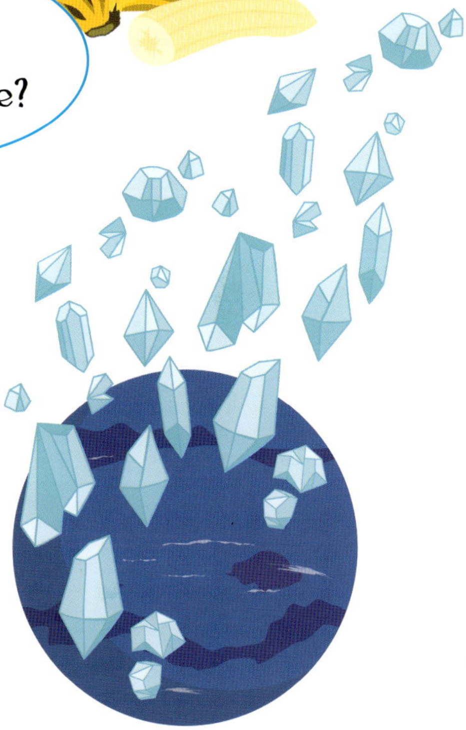

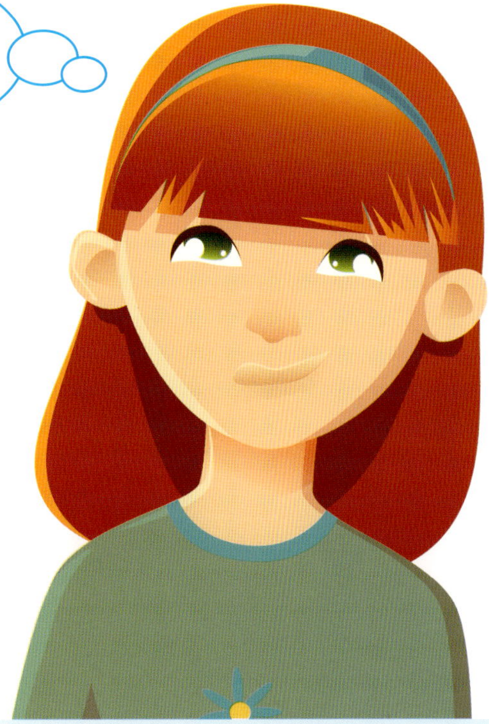

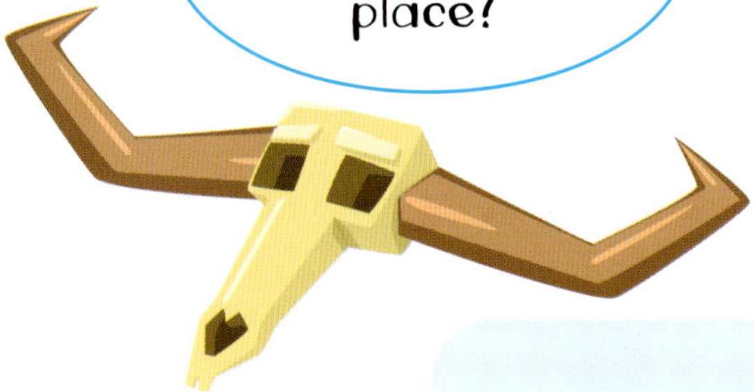

Where is the world's hottest place?

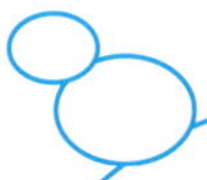

Where does it rain diamonds?

In this book, you'll find the answers to hundreds of smart science questions like these, on physics, chemistry, living things, the human body, space, and more.

Who knows, this book might be the first step to you becoming a brilliant brain surgeon or a rocket scientist!

WHAT IS EARTH'S MOST COMMON LIVING THING?

The planet belongs to bacteria, smaller than the eye can see.

How many bacteria are there?

There are a 100 million times more bacteria in the sea than there are stars in the Universe. Yet, we know very little about most of them.

What are bacteria?

Made up of just a single cell, bacteria are the simplest living creatures on the planet. Beastly bacteria cause disease, spoil food, and rot our teeth. But they also pump breathable oxygen into the air, help us digest our food, help plants to grow, and break down waste matter.

One drop of seawater can contain a million bacteria.

CAN ANYTHING SURVIVE IN BATTERY ACID?

Yes! Acid-loving microbes also live in hot springs, polluted mines—and your stomach!

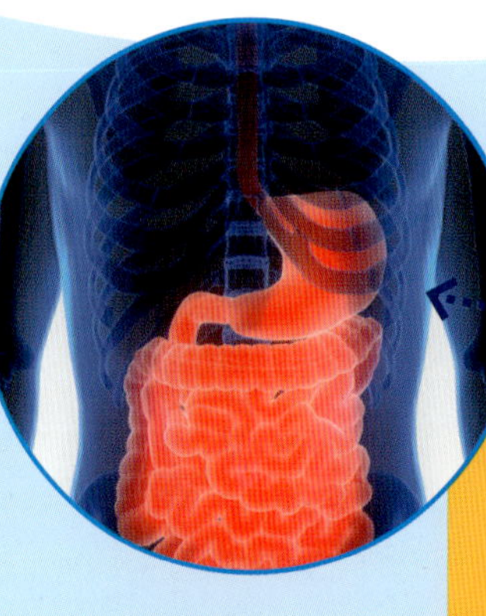

How tough are bacteria?

Some bacteria can thrive in very harsh conditions. These extreme organisms live in deadly hot and cold temperatures, soak up salt, dangerous radiation, and even bathe happily in acid. Scientists think they would have been tough enough to cope with conditions when Earth was young, and may have been some of the first lifeforms on the planet.

Which microbe passes the acid test?

Picrophilus holds the record for coping with acid. It even survives quite happily in 60 °C– (140 °F–) water, which can be more caustic (burning) than sulfuric acid.

Pollution from a mine.

WHERE DID LIFE BEGIN?

Scientists think they found the answer when they discovered life at the bottom of the ocean in 1977.

How can anything live here?

One of the great questions is how life began on our planet. When scientists discovered a thriving community of **organisms** (living things) near deep-sea vents, some of them wondered if life might have started here, far from the light of the Sun. It is thought that bacteria live off the chemical soup around the vents and that larger organisms, such as tubeworms, then feed on them.

What are the benefits of living by deep-sea vents?

All the raw materials to build life are found at deep-sea vents. Early organisms would also have been safe from the Sun's damaging radiation.

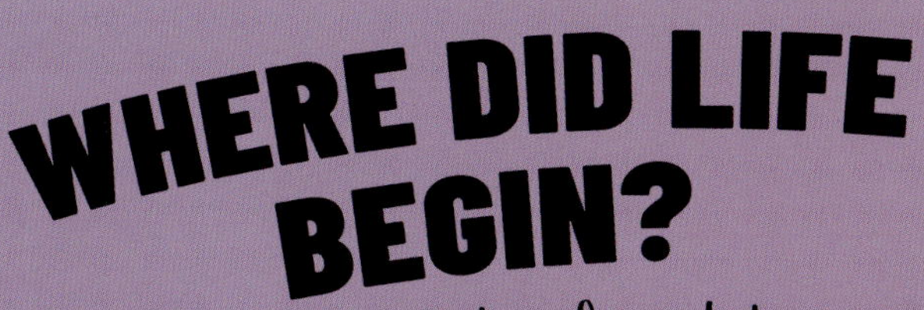

Bacteria have been around for at least 3.5 billion years.

HOW MANY NEW SPECIES ARE DISCOVERED EACH YEAR?

Thousands, and about half of them are insects!

Where are new species found?

Not all new species are found in the wild. Many are found in museum collections. In 2016, a new species of meat-eating plant was even identified in a picture on Facebook.

How many species are there?

Scientists think that there is space on the planet for 8.74 million different species, but around 7.5 million of these are yet to be discovered! More than 15,000 new species are found each year.

ARE THERE MORE INSECTS THAN PEOPLE ON EARTH?

There are 1.5 billion times more insects than people. Creepy-crawlies rule the planet!

What's the heaviest insect?

The giant **weta** is the world's heaviest insect. This scale-busting, 70- g (2.5- oz) bruiser is three times heavier than a mouse.

How many insects are there?

The six-legged creatures we call insects are the world's most successful animals. An estimated 10 quintillion (10,000,000,000,000,000,000) insects are alive today. There is no shortage of beetles. If you line up all of Earth's animals and plants in a row, then every fifth one would be a beetle.

For every person living on Earth there are about 1.4 million ants!

HOW FAST DO FLEAS TAKE OFF?

Fleas launch faster than a space rocket! These tiny, bloodsucking bugs have super-powered legs!

How high can a flea jump?

A flea clears 38 times its own body length. That's the same as a human hopping over four buses in a single jump.

Do fleas feel g-force?

These tiny biting beasties take off so fast they have to withstand 100 Gs—that's 100 times the force of gravity. The average g-force experienced by astronauts on board space rockets is around 3 Gs.

Leap like a flea

Time taken for a flea spring:
1/1000 second

Jump speed:
1.9 m (6.2 ft)/second

Average leap length:
7.6 cm (3 in)

WHAT IS THE WORLD'S SMELLIEST FLOWER?

The "corpse flower" may stink, but it makes up for that in size.

How big is it?

The **titan arum** is a truly strange flower. Towering 3 m (10 ft) high, it looks like a wrinkled finger sticking out of a paper cupcake case. Strictly speaking, it is many flowers attached to one tall stalk.

Why does it smell of rotting meat?

The smell would be unpleasant to us, but it attracts dung beetles and flesh flies in droves. They carry the titan arum's pollen!

WHERE DOES MOST OF OUR FOOD COME FROM?

Most of our food comes from plants. The staple diet of humans is surprisingly limited!

Should we vary our diet?

Humankind has cultivated crops that provide the highest output for the smallest area. As well as being quite boring, this tactic makes our food supplies vulnerable to climate change.

How many plants do we eat?

Plants make up more than four-fifths of our diet, yet we only eat about 30 different species. Nearly two-thirds of our food energy requirements are provided by just five crops—rice, wheat, maize, millet, and sorghum.

Is there anything else we can try?

If you're in the mood for something different, there are as many as 30,000 different species of edible plants to try.

WHAT ELSE ARE PLANTS USED FOR?

70,000 plant species are used to make cures for diseases or to relieve ailments.

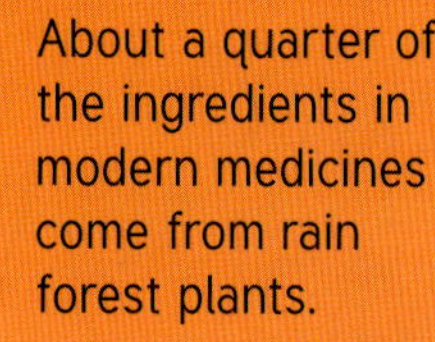

About a quarter of the ingredients in modern medicines come from rain forest plants.

What are herbal remedies?

Herbal remedies are made directly from plant extracts. These natural treatments tend to be traditional medicines used to treat everyday sicknesses, such as peppermint leaves to soothe an upset stomach.

Peppermint tea

Are all medicines from plants?

Modern medicines are **inorganic** (not living) chemicals made in a lab. Many of them are copied from nature. The headache drug aspirin contains an active ingredient first found in the bark of the willow tree.

IS A RAIN FOREST WET?

A rain forest is a place where at least 250 cm (98 in) of rain falls in a year, but some get double that amount.

How does the rain forest help the air?

The Amazon rain forest produces one-fifth of Earth's oxygen.

The Amazon rain forest is the biggest tropical rain forest in the world.

Rain forest

How many trees grow in the Amazon?

There are about 400 billion trees in the Amazon rain forest.

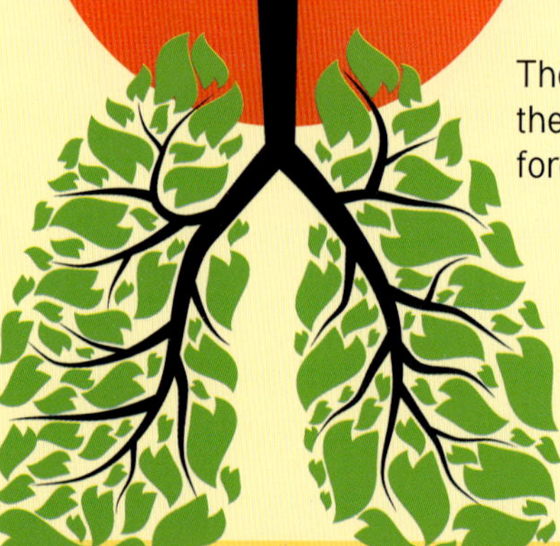

Are rain forests at risk?

An area of tropical rain forest greater than 45,000 soccer fields is destroyed every day.

WHAT IS THE WORLD'S LARGEST LIVING THING?

Blue whales have nothing on a giant American parasitic fungus.

How big is the super fungus?

The largest living thing on the planet is a honey fungus. Living in the Blue Mountains of Oregon, it is 3.8 km (2.4 miles) wide! When this branching beast meets up with genetically identical mushrooms, they merge together.

The yellow-brown mushrooms that pop up above ground are just the tip of this fungus iceberg. Most of the organism lives underground, in a spreading network of strings and tubes.

Can you eat honey fungus?

Apparently, honey fungus is delicious served on spaghetti!

Honey fungus

Which tree is the tallest?

The world's tallest tree is a lanky lunk redwood tree called Hyperion. It's 115.7 m (379.7 ft) tall—that's 21 m (70 ft) taller than the Statue of Liberty!

Giant redwood

Statue of Liberty

WHERE DO THE TALLEST LIVING THINGS GROW?

Northern California is home to the world's most tremendous trees.

Are they wide too?

Redwoods measure 7 m (24 ft) around their base. Giant sequoias are not as tall, but have much thicker trunks. "General Sherman" is 84 m (275 ft) tall, and measures a giant 31 m (102 ft) around its base.

Blue whale

How does the tallest tree compare to a blue whale?

Hyperion weighs an estimated 725,700 kg (1.6 million lbs)—that's more than three blue whales.

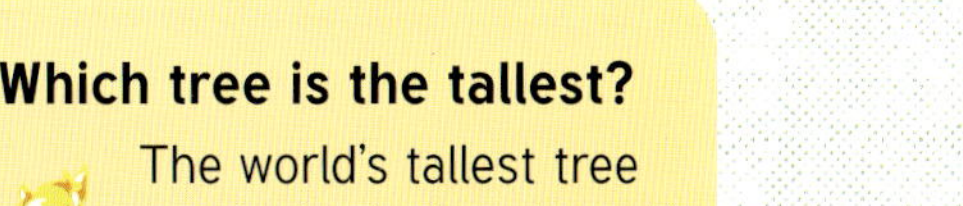

WHAT IS THE OLDEST LIVING THING ON EARTH?

The longest living organism is a bristlecone pine that was a youngster when the Ancient Egyptians started building pyramids.

Top three old-timers

Sacred fig tree
Country: Sri Lanka
Age: At least 2,222 years old

Patagonian cypress tree
Country: Chile
Age: 3,627 years old

Great Basin bristlecone pine
Country: USA
Age: 5,067 years old

Where does it grow?
The location of the oldest bristlecone pine is a well-kept secret, to stop it from becoming a tourist attraction.

HOW LONG CAN ANIMALS LIVE FOR?

The record for the oldest living thing goes to a clam called the ocean quahog.

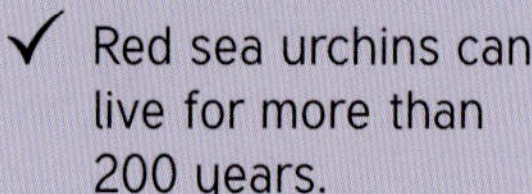

How old do quahogs get?
The **quahog** lives in the North Atlantic and grows to around 5 cm (2 in) across. No one knows exactly how long it can live, but one individual—called Ming—lived for 507 years!

- ✓ Red sea urchins can live for more than 200 years.
- ✓ Bowhead whales live for more than 200 years.
- ✓ One Greenland shark was known to have lived for more than 400 years.

How long do tortoises live for?
A tortoise called Tu'i Malila lived to the age of 189. Other tortoises may have lived longer!

HOW MUCH OF THE EARTH IS OCEAN?

Nearly three-quarters of Earth's surface is covered by oceans.

Plankton in the ocean provide most of the oxygen in our atmosphere.

What causes tides?

As the Moon orbits Earth, its gravity pulls seawater toward it, making two tides every day.

All five major oceans are connected to each other. The Pacific Ocean is the largest.

How are waves started?

Waves are created by winds blowing across the water.

Where are the highest tides?

The Bay of Fundy, between Nova Scotia and New Brunswick, in Canada, has the world's highest tides. They have a sea-level rise and fall of 16.3 m (53.5 ft).

Is the world's longest mountain range underwater?

Yes. The world's longest mountain range stretches 65,000 km (40,389 miles) through the middle of the oceans.

The name of the Pacific Ocean is taken from Latin, and it means "peaceful."

Is the sea full of treasure?

There are about 20 million tonnes (22 million tons) of gold dissolved in the oceans.

Are there many shipwrecks?

There may be as many as 3 million shipwrecks littering the ocean floors.

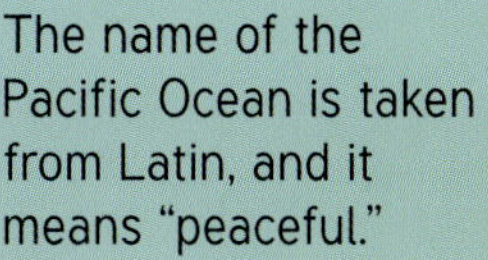

WHERE DO MOST THINGS LIVE?

Life started out in the oceans, and most of it stayed there!

How much life is in the seas?

Scientists say that 99 percent of the living space on Earth is in the sea. So it's no surprise to learn that 94 percent of organisms live there. What is surprising is that we have only met a fraction of them.

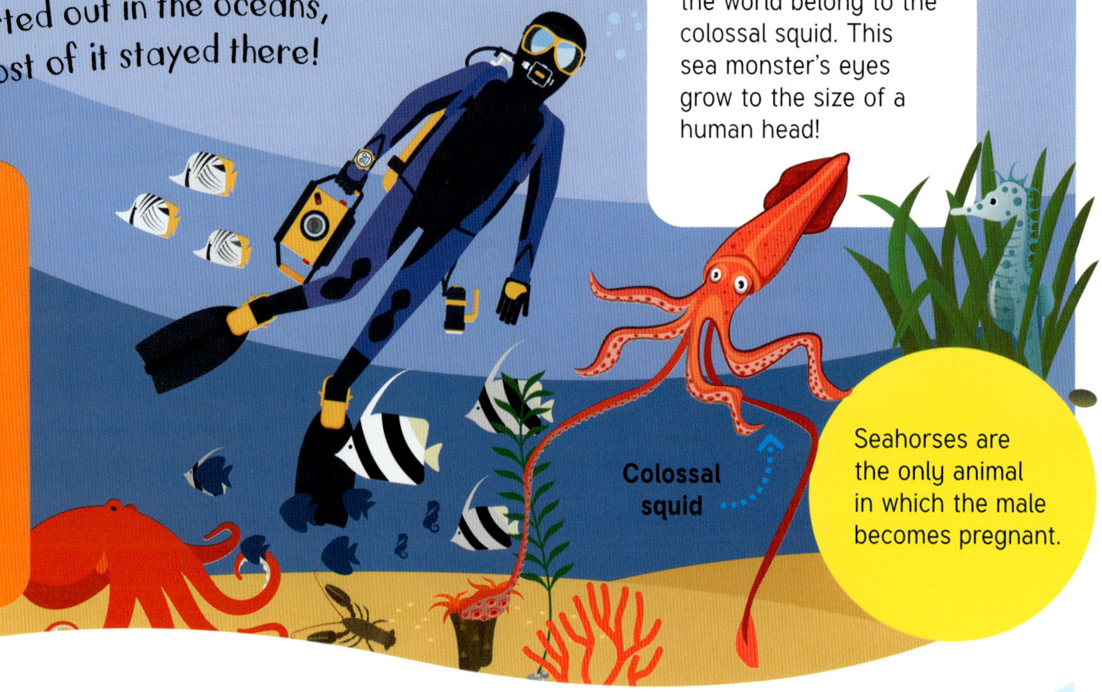

Which animal has the biggest eyes?

The biggest eyes in the world belong to the colossal squid. This sea monster's eyes grow to the size of a human head!

Seahorses are the only animal in which the male becomes pregnant.

DOES THE SEA GLOW?

Ancient sailors called it "the burning of the sea"—eerie blue lights that appear on dark nights in places where seawater is disturbed.

The scientific word for glowing creatures is **bioluminescence** (say bye-oh-loom-min-ess-ents).

What causes the glowing in the oceans?

Many sea creatures create light, but microscopic plankton produce the weirdest effect. Tiny neon pinpricks of light look like a floating field of stars. Scientists think these light signals act like a burglar alarm, alerting big animals to the presence of the plankton's predators. Larger predators then arrive to feed on the plankton's enemies.

Are glowing sea creatures common?

More than four in five ocean animals have the ability to produce light.

WHERE DO YOU FIND KILLER ICICLES?

Strange fingers of death called "brinicles" creep down through freezing water in the Arctic and Antarctic, killing everything in their path. This is how it happens:

1 Polar air temperatures hover around -20 °C (-4 °F), but seawater is -1.9 °C (-28.58 °F). Heat moves from the warmer water to the air. Sea ice forms at the surface.

2 Salt is excluded as ice crystals form. Salt-heavy brine builds up in cracks and channels within the sea ice.

3 The concentrated brine sinks. It is now below the freezing point of seawater, since salt-rich water freezes at lower temperatures.

4 Seawater drawn toward the brine freezes instantly, killing nearby creatures with its extreme cold.

HOW NOISY IS THE OCEAN?

Dip a hydrophone (underwater microphone) into the water to hear the seas' spookiest sounds.

Which animal is the loudest?

The blue whale's song is the loudest sound made by an animal. Its 188-decibels solo effort can be heard 800 km (500 miles) away.

What is the Bloop?

Mystery sounds in the ocean are given unusual names. "The Bloop" was a powerful, ultra-low-frequency sound, picked up in 1997 by listening stations thousands of miles apart. It may have been caused by an underwater icequake, a volcanic eruption, or an iceberg, but if the source was an animal, it would be bigger than a blue whale.

HOW DEEP IS THE SEA?

The ocean is 3.7 km (2.3 miles) deep on average. That's about eight Empire State Buildings, stacked on top of each other.

Empire State Building

Where is the ocean deepest?

The deepest point in the ocean is the Mariana Trench, about 300 km (190 miles) southwest of Guam in the Pacific Ocean.

Mount Everest would comfortably fit into the Mariana Trench, with a mile or so to spare.

How deep does it get?

Challenger Deep, part of the Mariana Trench, is 11,030 m (36,200 ft) deep. That's the height of 25 stacked Empire State Buildings.

More is known about the surface of the Moon than the depths of the ocean.

Goblin shark

Is it dark in the depths?

Light does not reach farther than 1 km (3,280 ft) undersea. Zones deeper than this are pitch black.

Anglerfish

What about water pressure?

Animals at the bottom of the ocean survive pressures of 1 tonne (1.1 tons) on each 1 cm^2 (0.15 in^2) of their bodies.

Mysterious undersea "rivers" carrying sand and silt run along the ocean floor.

Is it cold at the bottom?

Deep ocean water is 0–3 °C (32–37 °F).

A whale carcass can support a whole community of organisms for decades.

IS CHALK MADE FROM DEAD CREATURES?

The famous, towering white cliffs of England, France, and Denmark are made from mini fossils smaller than the eye can see!

How was chalk made?

Chalk was once a fine mud on the seabed. This gungy ooze was made from the microscopic remains of tiny plankton that had sunk to the bottom when they died.

Here are some of the **microfossils you can find in chalk:**

- Forams
- Ostracods
- Diatoms
- Dinoflagellates
- Coccoliths
- Radiolarians

How old is chalk?

Most chalk was laid down in the Cretaceous period, between 100 and 60 million years ago.

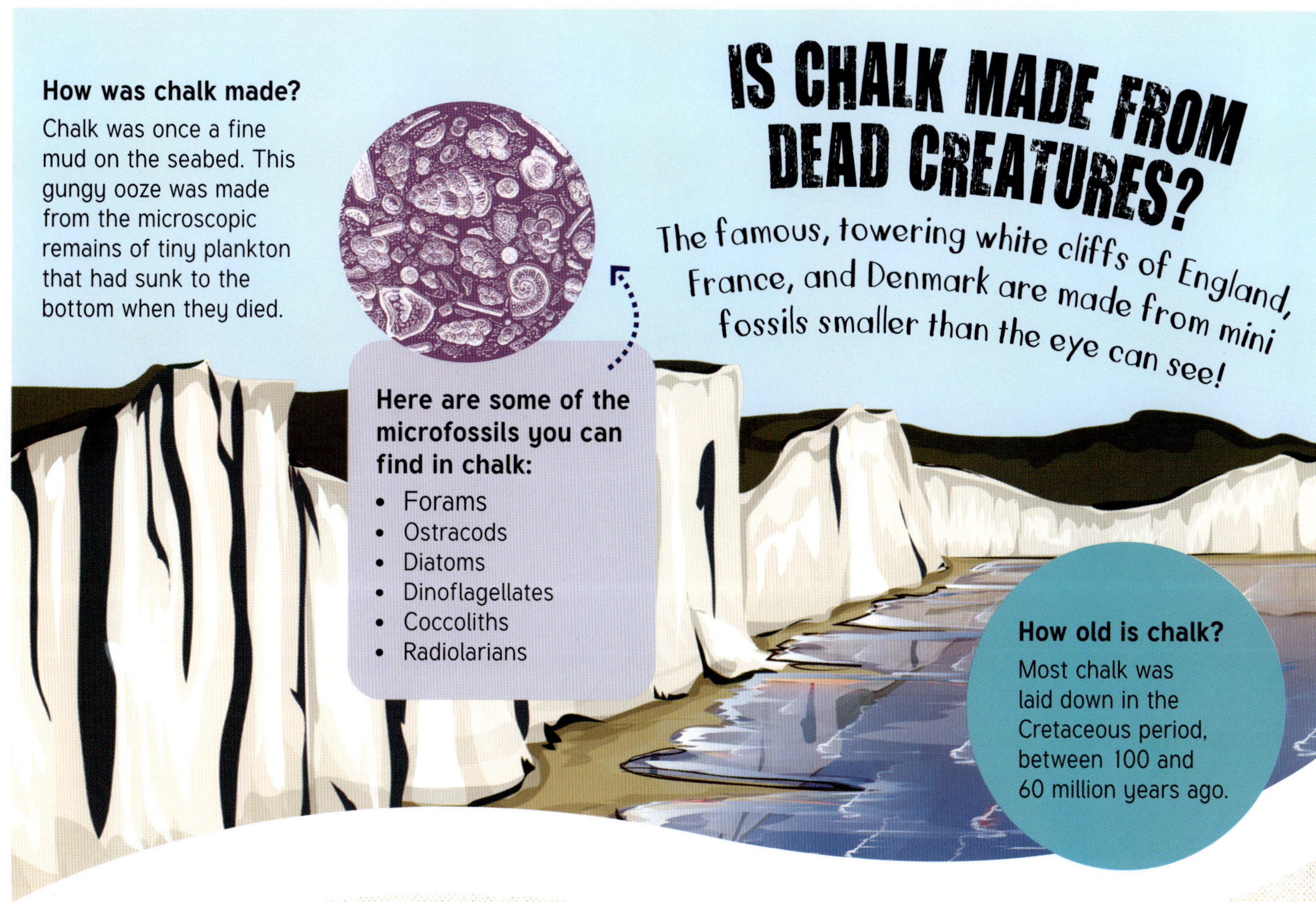

WERE PREHISTORIC INSECTS BIGGER THAN BIRDS?

Yes, 300 million years ago there was a giant dragonfly buzzing about!

Why did insects grow so large?

High oxygen levels in the Carboniferous period boosted insect sizes. Some of the fearsome frights that lived at the time include a millipede that was 2.3 m (7.5 ft) long—longer than a king-sized bed!

How big was it?

Less fly and more dragon, **Meganeura** measured around 65 cm (26 in) from wingtip to wingtip. That's roughly the same as a pigeon! Like today's dragonflies, Meganeura laid its eggs in water and probably spent most of its life as a larva in the water.

DID STEGOSAURUS HAVE A TINY BRAIN?

Stegosaurus may have had giant tail-spikes, but its brain was no bigger than a walnut!

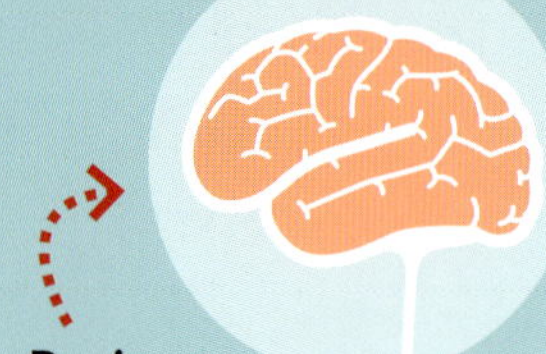

Why was its brain so small?

Many dinosaurs had small brains, because much of the space in their skulls was used to anchor powerful biting muscles. Although its brain was the same size as a walnut, it was shaped more like a sausage.

How did Stegosaurus get its name?

Stegosaurus means "roofed lizard," because paleontologists first thought the dino's plates were like roofing tiles.

When did Stegosaurus live?

Stegosaurus lived during the late Jurassic Period, about 155-150 million years ago.

WHAT IS A VERTEBRATE?

Vertebrates are animals with backbones. This group includes fish, amphibians, reptiles, mammals, and birds.

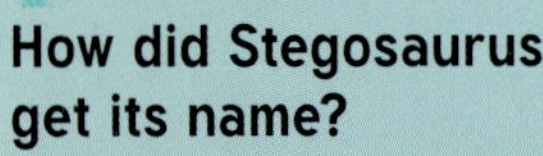

What was the first vertebrate?

Animals with backbones evolved in the sea during the Cambrian period, about 500 million years ago. The first vertebrates looked like worms. These mini-wrigglers, smaller than a paper clip, swam free in the ancient oceans. They may not look much like us, but just like all animals with backbones, these Cambrian critters have top-to-bottom symmetrical bodies and blocks of muscles attached to the spine to move them about.

Are the first vertebrates still around?

No, but one modern creature looks remarkably similar to these ancient ancestors. The **lancelet** lives half-buried in sand on riverbeds, and resembles Myllokunmingia.

HOW MANY ICE AGES WERE THERE?

There have been at least five significant ice ages in Earth's history.

During the most recent Ice Age, snow and ice permanently covered huge parts of the planet.

How long did they last?

The last Ice Age lasted about 100,000 years, between 110,000 to 12,000 years ago.

Woolly mammoth

Large animals hold their body heat better than smaller ones, and fare better during cold periods.

How long were mammoth tusks?

A woolly mammoth's tusks were about 2.7 m (8.9 ft) long and weighed about 45 kg (99 lbs)—that's as heavy as four gold bars!

What was the largest ever land mammal?

Paraceratherium, was a 20-tonne (22-ton) giant, hornless rhino.

Could we bring back mammoths?

Scientists aim to bring mammoths back to life by putting their frozen DNA into elephant embryos.

Are there mammoths in ice?

Many woolly mammoth bodies have been found intact, buried in permafrost (frozen soil).

Were there Ice Age rhinos?

Yes. One furry Ice Age rhino had a wide, flat horn for shovelling snow.

Megacerops

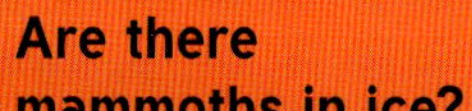

Dire wolves were huge wolves. Their shaggy bodies were found trapped in tar pits in California.

Titanis

Many enormous animals lived during the Ice Age. They are known as **megafauna**.

DO HUMANS HAVE SUPERSIZED BRAINS?

Yes, they are unusually large for our body size.

How many brain cells do we have?

16.3 billion

When did humans get bigger brains?

Around 2.5 million years ago, our ancestors' brains got bigger. Fossils show that the brains of these early humans went from 0.6 l (20 fl oz)—about two soft drink cans—to about 1 l (2 pints). This gave early humans a boost in intelligence.

How many brain cells do elephants have?

5.59 billion

Why aren't animals with bigger brains smarter?

Intelligence isn't just about big brains. Elephants and whales have much bigger brains than humans, but we have many more brain cells in the thinking parts of our brains.

HOW LONG CAN HUMANS EXPECT TO LIVE?

On average, humans live to be 71 and a half years old, but some people knock this average out of the park!

Who was the oldest human?

Jeanne Calment had the longest human life ever recorded. The French supercentenarian was born in 1875 and died in 1997, aged 122 years and 164 days.

Which country has the oldest population?

With people living longer and fewer babies being born, some nations are actually getting older. In Japan, the number of people aged 60+ has quadrupled in the last 40 years.

HOW MANY PEOPLE LIVE ON OUR PLANET?

Just over 100 years ago, there were only one billion people living on Earth. Today there are more than 8 billion.

This is where most people on Earth live: *

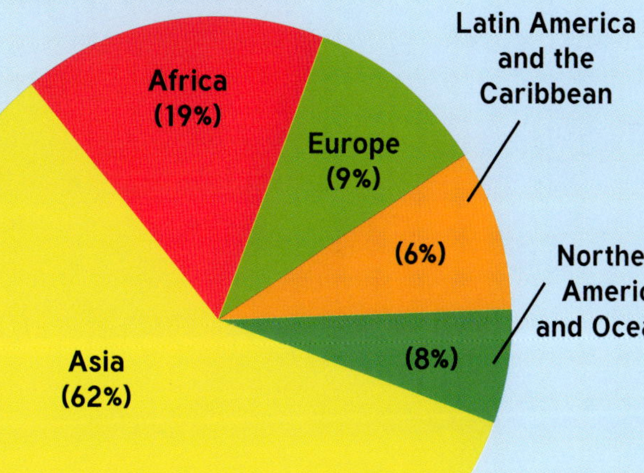

Which countries have the most people?

The country with the most people is India. About 1.44 billion people live there. China is next, with 1.43 billion people.

*The numbers in this chart add up to more than 100% because of rounding.

How is the population growing?

Compared to 60 years ago, women have many fewer children. However, those babies are much more likely to survive to become adults. This means the world's population is still growing!

HOW MANY KIDS ARE ON EARTH?

There are 1.8 billion young people in the world aged between 10 and 24—more than there has ever been.

Which country has the youngest population?

Niger, in Africa.

How fast is the population growing?

250 babies are born every minute.

COULD ALL THE HUMANS ON THE PLANET SQUEEZE INTO ONE CITY?

The entire world's population could fit within the American city of Los Angeles. Imagine—7.6 billion people squeezed into just 1,300 km² (500 mi²). There would be no way you could see the sights!

How squeezed could you get?

Why stop there? The atoms of our bodies are mostly empty space. If you could find a way to extract it and squeeze a person into the smallest possible volume ... the whole human race would fit into a space the size of a sugar cube!

WHERE DO OVER HALF THE PEOPLE ON EARTH LIVE?

The largest percentage of people live in cities. Cities occupy a tiny amount of the available land on Earth. However, more than half of us live in one. One out of every five people lives in a large city with a population greater than 1 million. There are more than 30 mega cities, with over 10 million people.

Where is the largest city?

Tokyo-Yokohama, Japan, is the largest urban area in the world. It is home to over 37 million people.

Ten of the world's top 20 fastest-growing cities are in China.

Where is the most crowded?

Macau in China is the most crowded city in the world, with nearly 20,500 people/km² (53,330 people/mi²).

HOW OLD IS OUR SOLAR SYSTEM?

The Sun and the planets orbiting it are 4.6 billion years old. Scientists think that they were created when a nearby star exploded.

1. Take a dust cloud floating in space and set off a massive explosion close by (an exploding star does the trick).

2. The cloud collapses in on itself and gets more and more dense.

3. When enough stuff is squeezed together in the middle, nuclear fusion reactions begin and a new star is born.

4. The new star is surrounded by a flat, spinning disk of leftover debris. Planets form out of this material to create a solar system!

WHERE IS MOST OF OUR SOLAR SYSTEM?

Almost all of the Solar System's mass is found in the huge star in the middle.

How big is the Sun?
The Sun is really big, amazingly so. More than a million Earths could fit inside our star.

How much of the Solar System is the Sun?
Our Sun contains 99.86 percent of all matter in our Solar System. Everything else—all the planets and moons, as well as the countless asteroids, comets, and other amazing objects in our solar system—is made from the 0.14 percent left.

How about Jupiter?
Most of the material that makes up that tiny 0.14 percent of leftovers is in Jupiter. Together with Saturn, it makes up more than 90 percent of the mass of all the planets.

WILL THE OCEANS BOIL AWAY?

In just 2 billion years, the Sun will get so hot that Earth's oceans will evaporate. It's just one effect of our star getting older.

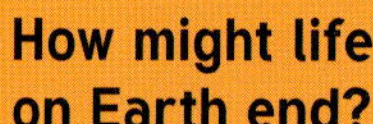

How long will the Sun last?

The life span of a star like our Sun is about 10 billion years. This means that it is already about halfway through its life.

How might life on Earth end?

As the Sun's core runs out of hydrogen, it will start burning up heavier fuel, growing brighter and hotter as a result. Two billion years from now, the Earth will be so hot that the water in our oceans will boil away. This will be the end of life on Earth and our planet will become a desert world, similar to Mars today.

WHICH PLANET IS THE FASTEST?

Mercury. By the time Earth has looped around the Sun once, speedy Mercury has whizzed around it more than four times!

Why is Mercury so fast?

Mercury is the closest planet to the Sun, so its journey around the Sun is the shortest. This tiny, rocky planet is also held more tightly by the Sun's powerful gravity. It has to travel faster to balance the pull from the Sun.

Speedy Mercury facts

- Mercury's average speed is 170,505 km/h (106,000 mph).
- Mercury circles the Sun in just 88 Earth-days.

ARE EARTH DAYS GETTING LONGER?

Earth days are getting longer as the Moon's gravity gently slows our planet's rotation.

How fast are we moving?

You are moving through space at around 107,200 km/h (67,000 mph)—that's about 100 times faster than a passenger jet.

How long is a Moon orbit?

It takes approximately 27 days for the Moon to orbit (circle) the Earth.

Is the Moon leaving Earth?

The Moon is slowly drifting away from Earth, at about the same speed that your fingernails grow.

Which planet is the densest?

Earth is the densest planet in the Solar System.

How hot is the Earth's core?

The temperature of Earth's core is around 6,000 °C (10,800 °F)—as hot as the Sun's surface.

How did the Moon form?

Scientists think that the Moon formed when a Mars-sized space rock smashed into Earth around 4.5 billion years ago.

Amazingly, the Moon is exactly the same size in the sky as the Sun. Our star is about 400 times wider than our Moon, but is around 400 times farther away.

Why do we only see one side of the Moon?

A day on the Moon lasts as long as its year. Because our satellite spins at precisely the same speed as it orbits Earth, we only ever see one side of the Moon.

Would we be lighter on the Moon?

Gravity on the Moon is about a sixth of what it is on Earth. Visit the Moon and you instantly lose five-sixths of your weight!

WHICH IS THE HOTTEST PLANET?

Venus is nearly twice as far from the Sun as Mercury, but it is actually hotter.

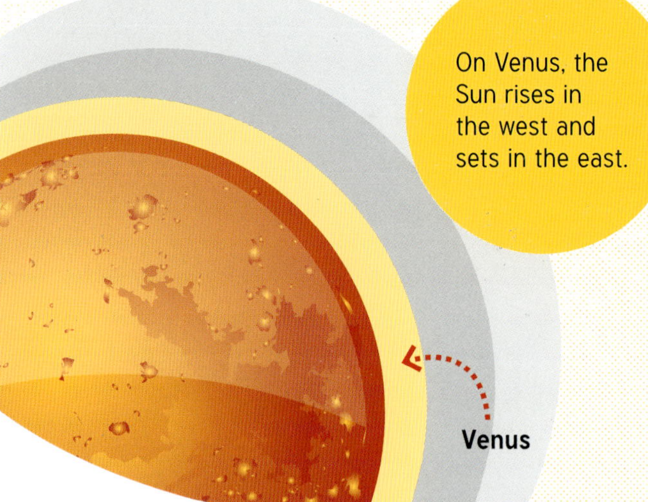

On Venus, the Sun rises in the west and sets in the east.

Is Venus like Earth?

Venus is sometimes called our "sister planet" because it is almost exactly the same size as Earth. But the similarity ends there! Venus has a dense atmosphere of carbon dioxide. Clouds of deadly sulfuric acid fill the sky. The air is so thick that the pressure at the surface is a crushing 90 times higher than on Earth.

How hot is Venus?

Venus' dense atmosphere traps the Sun's heat, raising the surface temperature to over 462 °C (864 °F). That's hot enough to melt tin and lead.

WHICH PLANET IS A SIGHTSEER'S DREAM?

Mars has many of the Solar System's most amazing sights.

Does Mars have a Grand Canyon?

The 4,000- km (2,500- miles) long Valles Marineris puts the USA's Grand Canyon to shame. This massive rift in the planet's surface is 7 km (4 miles) deep at its lowest point.

Where is the Solar System's biggest volcano?

Olympus Mons, on Mars, is the largest volcano in our Solar System. This mountain of rock is 600 km (370 miles) across and towers 22 km (14 miles) high. That's two-and-a-half times as tall as the highest mountain on Earth. Scientists think the volcano may still be active.

HOW MUCH BIGGER THAN EARTH IS JUPITER?

Jupiter is 1,000 times bigger than Earth and everything about it is jumbo-sized.

Jupiter

What is Jupiter's Great Red Spot?

The **Great Red Spot** on Jupiter is a gigantic storm, similar to a tropical cyclone. The main difference compared to a hurricane on Earth is that Jupiter's version is unbelievably huge—three times the size of our planet!

How long has Jupiter had its spot?

With no solid ground to slow them down, storms on Jupiter blow for a very long time. The Great Red Spot was first spotted in 1830 and it has been raging since then, but it may have been blowing for 350 years or more!

WHICH PLANET HAS THE MOST MOONS?

Of all the planets in the Solar System, Jupiter has the largest number of moons, with a total of 95. The next planet with lots of moons is Uranus, with 28.

The four largest moons of Jupiter are called the **Galilean moons**. These icy worlds were discovered by the famous Italian scientist Galileo in 1610.

1 **Io** bubbles over with volcanoes, which shoot out fountains of lava and plumes of icy sulfur into space.

Io

3 **Ganymede**, the Solar System's largest moon, is bigger than Mercury.

4 Pockmarked with craters, **Callisto** is a dead world that looks much like our own Moon.

2 Mini **Europa** is covered in sheets of ice. However, scientists think a liquid ocean where life may lurk lies beneath its frozen surface.

Europa

COULD SATURN FLOAT IN WATER?

Yes! Saturn may be the Solar System's second-largest planet, but it is made of light gases.

Could you stand on Saturn?

You can't stand on Saturn. It is made of hydrogen and helium (the same light gas that goes into party balloons). Those gases are lighter than water, meaning Saturn would float. But who has a tub big enough?

What are Saturn's rings made of?

Saturn's rings are enormous, but very thin, at less than 1 km (0.6 miles) thick. They are not solid, but are made of dust, rocks, and chunks of ice—some as big as houses.

WAS URANUS NEARLY CALLED GEORGE?

Yes! Here's the story of how Uranus got its funny name.

1781 Uranus is discovered by English astronomer William Herschel. It has been spotted before, but has always been mistaken for a star. Using a telescope, he realizes it is a planet.

1783 Herschel calls his discovery "Georgium Sidus" after King George III. In 1783, "George" is recognized as a planet.

1850 The other planets in our solar system are named after gods from Greek mythology. Johann Bode changes its name to "Uranus"—after the Greek god of the sky.

What's odd about Uranus' orbit?

Uranus orbits the Sun on its side.

WHERE DOES IT RAIN DIAMONDS?

Neptune is the king of bling. On this icy giant planet, uncut diamond "hailstones" rain from the sky.

How does diamond rain form?

Neptune is a frozen world far, far away from the Sun. Its atmosphere contains lots of frozen methane. On Earth this is the natural gas we burn in boilers, heaters, and ovens in the home. But squeezed in the dense atmosphere of Neptune, it turns into solid diamonds, leading to extremely hard rain showers!

What is Neptune's weather like?

Neptune has the strongest winds in the Solar System. Frozen methane clouds whip across the skies at speeds of more than 2,000 km/h (1,200 mph).

HOW PUNY IS PLUTO?

Pluto is 2,370 km (1,473 miles) wide. This means that it could easily fit onto the landmass of the USA, which is about 4,669 km (2,800 miles) wide.

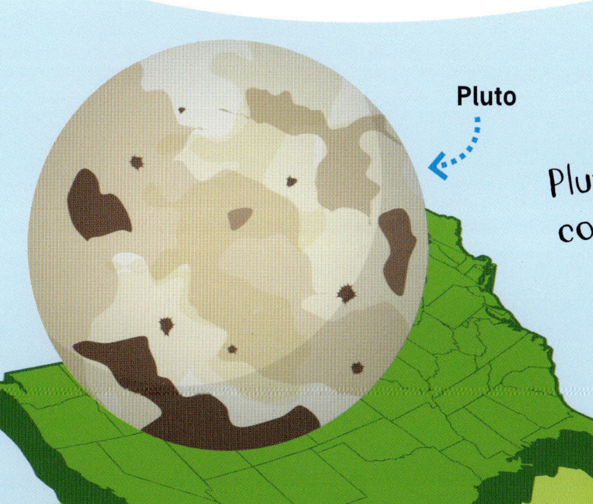

How do we know Pluto's size?

NASA's New Horizons spacecraft flew by Pluto in 2015, and took the first accurate measurements of this dwarf planet.

Why was Pluto downgraded?

In 2006, Pluto lost its status as a planet. Because it lacks the bulk to sweep its orbit clean of space rocks and other debris, it was demoted to the status of dwarf planet.

Could you walk around Pluto?

A hike around Pluto's equator would be 7,445 km (4,627 miles)— roughly the same distance as from Anchorage, Alaska, to Mexico City.

WHICH ASTRONAUTS WENT THE FARTHEST?

The Apollo 13 crew set the record for going farthest from Earth: 400,171 km (248,655 miles).

Which animal was first into space?

Fruit flies were the first living things sent into space. They went up in 1947.

Is space smelly?

Astronauts report that space smells like seared steak, hot metal, and welding fumes. Yummy!

Which animal was first to orbit Earth?

The first living thing to orbit Earth was a Russian dog called **Laika** in 1957.

The **Voyager 1** probe left the Solar System in 2013 and is still journeying.

How long could you survive in space?

You couldn't survive in space without a spacesuit for more than 30 seconds.

Who has spent the longest time in space?

Russia's Valeri Polyakov holds the record for the longest stay in space: 437 days and 18 hours.

Do astronauts grow in space?

Astronauts get taller in space. The spine expands when it's not being pulled down by Earth's gravity.

Do astronauts drink pee?

Astronauts on the *International Space Station* drink their own (recycled) sweat, breath, and even pee!

Astronauts in orbit around Earth see a fresh sunrise every 90 minutes.

WHAT IS IN THE MIDDLE OF OUR GALAXY?

There's a black hole in the middle of the Solar System, a place in space where gravity is so strong that not even light can escape.

Black holes come in three sizes:

Tiny tykes

As big as a single atom, but containing more mass than a mountain.

Dark stars

Star-sized black holes form when dying stars collapse. They have ten times the Sun's mass in a space the size of New York City.

Are black holes empty?

No, they contain a huge amount of material squeezed into a tiny space. Because light cannot escape their gravity, they are invisible—but they can be detected by their effect on matter nearby.

Supersize!

Supermassive black holes are giants with the mass of a million Suns. Our galaxy has one at its heart.

IS OUR GALAXY ON A COLLISION COURSE?

Yes. In 4 billion years the Milky Way will crash into the Andromeda Galaxy.

Will there be a huge explosion?

Rather than a sudden crash, the galaxies will gently merge. As the distances between stars are so large, hardly any will actually collide. However, future astronomers will be able to enjoy a billion-year-long light show.

How fast are the galaxies moving together?

402,000 km/h (249,791 mph)

How far apart are we now?

Our galaxy, the Milky Way, and the the large spiral galaxy Andromeda are currently about 2.5 million light years apart. Drawn by each other's enormous gravity, they are hurtling toward each other at a blistering speed of more than 100,000 m (328,000 ft) per second.

CAN STARS EXPLODE?

A star explodes in the Universe every second, going BOOM! at the end of its life. These spectacular explosions are called **supernovas**.

Will the Sun explode?

No. Our star is not massive enough to go supernova.

Supernova

What happens in a supernova?

In the first 10 seconds of a supernova explosion, a dying star produces more energy than our Sun will release in its 10-billion-year lifetime. For a short time, a single star burns with more energy than a whole galaxy!

How often do supernovas happen in our galaxy?

Dying stars go out in a blaze of glory. They burn brightly for weeks, looking like a new star appearing in the night sky. In a galaxy the size of the Milky Way, a supernova happens about once every 50 years.

Pulsar

CAN SUPERNOVAS FORM NEW STARS?

Pulsars are a type of neutron star— the remnants of a gigantic supernova explosion.

How are pulsars formed?

When a massive star explodes in a supernova, its core collapses inward to form a new, super-dense neutron star. Neutron stars send a beam of radio waves out of each pole. When seen from Earth, this beam blinks on and off like a lighthouse, as the star spins around.

When were pulsars discovered?

Jocelyn Bell discovered the first **pulsar** in 1967. Scientists thought that the pulsar's flickering signal might have been a sign from aliens.

How heavy is a neutron star?

A teaspoonful of neutron stars would weigh 5.4 billion tonnes (6 billion tons).

HOW DID THE UNIVERSE BEGIN?

Scientists think that everything began with a bang 13.8 billion years ago! All the matter in the Universe exploded out of a tiny dot.

How do we know this happened?

This surprising idea, that the Universe expanded in a hyper-hot explosion, has three key things going for it:

1 All galaxies are moving away from each other. The farthest galaxies are moving the fastest. This happens in explosions.

2 Heat left over from a colossal ancient explosion can still be detected in all areas of the sky.

3 The amounts of hydrogen and helium in the Universe are as predicted by the Big Bang theory.

CAN WE LOOK BACK IN TIME?

The farther away objects are in space, the older they are.

How can we see the past?

Light from stars takes time to travel across space and arrive at our eyes. So, we never see a star as it is right now. We always see it as it was a long time ago.

How old is the sunlight we see?

It takes light 8 minutes and 19 seconds to travel from the Sun to Earth. If the Sun suddenly shut down, we wouldn't notice until about eight-and-a-third minutes later. The nearest star to the Sun, **Proxima Centauri**, is 4.25 light-years away. That means it takes 4.25 years for light to travel from Proxima Centauri to Earth.

WHAT TURNS A COMPASS NEEDLE?

Pull out a compass and watch as the needle swings toward the North Pole. You are picking up Earth's unseen magnetic field.

What makes Earth magnetic?

Earth's inner core is mostly solid iron, but it is surrounded by a churning outer core of liquid iron. The molten metal creates electrical currents, and these in turn generate an enormous magnetic field.

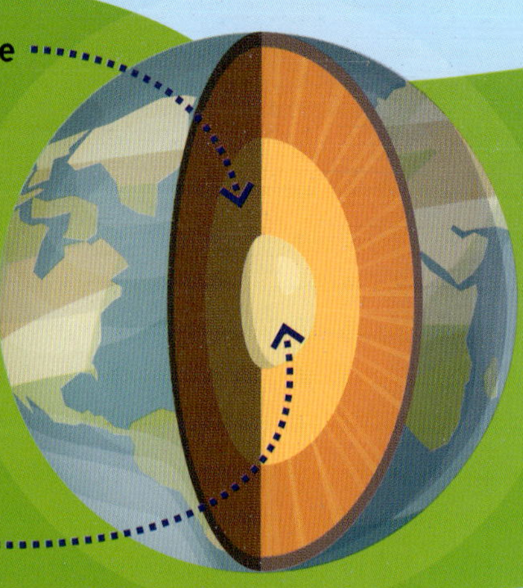

How does the magnetic field protect us?

Earth's magnetic field extends into space. This invisible forcefield protects us from dangerous charged particles streaming from the Sun.

Is there more than one North Pole?

The actual North Pole (Earth's most northerly point) and the **Magnetic North Pole** (where a compass needle points) are not in the same place. The magnetic pole moves around, but they are currently about 500 km (310 miles) apart.

DOES THE EARTH SPIN FASTER AT THE EQUATOR THAN AT THE POLES?

Yes. This fact is a head-scratcher. How does the planet avoid unscrewing itself?

How does this happen?

Because Earth is ball-shaped, it is widest around its middle. The planet rotates on its axis once every day. To make a full turn, an object on Earth's equator has to travel farther than something near the poles. Since a day lasts the same time on all parts of the planet, the equator must turn faster to keep up.

How fast does the Earth spin?

The distance around the planet's equator is roughly 40,000 km (24,855 miles) and Earth completes one full rotation every 24 hours. At the equator, an object spins at a dizzying 1,664 km/h (1,000 mph).

IS THE EARTH LIKE A JIGSAW PUZZLE?

Earth's crust has eight major plates and many smaller plates, which fit together like a jigsaw puzzle.

How often do earthquakes happen?

Millions of earthquakes occur each year, but only about 100 of them cause damage.

Do the plates move?

The plates move at about the same speed as your fingernails grow. Most earthquakes are triggered when plates move.

What causes tsunamis?

Tsunamis are caused by underwater earthquakes. Ocean swells travel at nearly 1,000 km/h (600 mph), and when they hit land, waves over 30 m (100 ft) high cause devastating destruction.

Where are most of Earth's volcanoes?

Over three-quarters of Earth's volcanoes are on the rim of the Pacific Ocean, called the "Ring of Fire."

How fast do volcanoes form?

Volcanoes can form quickly. In 1943, Parícutin in Mexico grew into a five-story-high hill in a week. By the end of the year it was 336 m (1,102 ft) tall.

How many volcanoes are there?

There are around 1,500 active volcanoes today, and nearly one in 10 people live within the danger zone of an active volcano.

In Japanese mythology, a giant catfish called **Namazu** causes earthquakes when he slaps his mighty tail.

How long do earthquakes last?

The longest quake ever recorded was the 2004 Indian Ocean earthquake, which lasted 10 minutes.

WHERE IS THE "DEATH ZONE"?

Above 8,000 m (26,250 ft) on mountain peaks, there is barely enough oxygen in the air to breathe.

Why do climbers carry oxygen?

The lack of pressure up on the "roof of the world" means that the body does not take in enough oxygen. This causes altitude sickness, which has symptoms that include headaches, nausea, and problems with thinking straight. This can be dangerous, which is why climbers often use oxygen tanks at these heights.

Can you climb the highest mountains without oxygen?

Inside the "death zone," most climbers carry oxygen tanks. However, some climbers still make ascents without oxygen.

WHAT IS THE TALLEST MOUNTAIN?

This might come as a surprise! Mauna Kea on Hawaii's Big Island is officially the world's tallest mountain, if we measure from its underwater base to peak.

How tall is Mauna Kea?

When measured from its base on the seabed, Mauna Kea is 10,200 m (33,456 ft) tall.

WHERE IS MOST OF EARTH'S ATMOSPHERE?

Two-thirds of Earth's atmosphere is within 8 km (5 miles) of Earth's surface.

How heavy is a cloud?

An average cloud weighs the same as 80 elephants.

Where does space begin?

The official boundary of space is 100 km (62 miles) above Earth's surface.

Where does the weather happen?

Earth's weather occurs in the thickest layer of the atmosphere, closest to the ground.

What are jet streams?

These are speedy air currents that blast around the globe at speeds up to 321 km/h (200 mph).

How heavy is the atmosphere?

You don't feel it, but you have 1 tonne (1.1 tons) of air pressing down on you.

Why is ozone important?

Ozone is a blue gas with a strong smell. At ground level it is pollution, but high in the sky it protects the planet from damaging UV radiation.

How is the greenhouse effect bad news?

The greenhouse effect keeps the planet warm enough for life to exist. However, global temperature is increasing, thanks to the extra greenhouse gases added by burning fossil fuels such as petroleum and natural gas.

What is the greenhouse effect?

The thick blanket of atmospheric gas around the planet traps the Sun's energy.

Are there benefits to greenhouse gases?

Without the effect of greenhouse gases, such as carbon dioxide, Earth's heat would be lost to space.

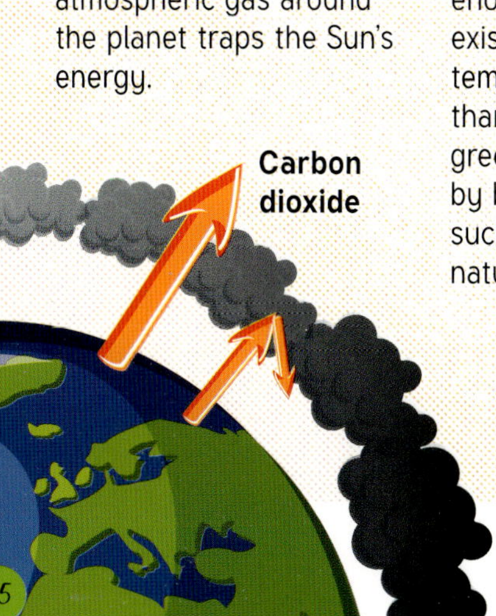

WHAT ARE THE NORTHERN LIGHTS?

Dancing lights above Earth's poles reveal the planet's magnetic secrets.

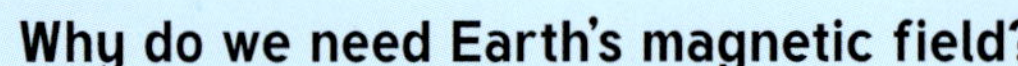

What causes the lights?

The northern and southern lights hang like shimmering curtains in the skies close to Earth's poles. Called **auroras**, they are made when fast-moving protons and electrons smash into gas molecules in the upper atmosphere, causing the gases to glow.

Why do we need Earth's magnetic field?

Our star constantly hurls energetic particles into space. This "solar wind" would destroy our atmosphere and wipe out life, were it not for Earth's magnetic field. This invisible forcefield protects the planet by pushing away or trapping most of the particles and cosmic rays.

WHAT TIME IS IT AT EARTH'S POLES?

At the North and South Pole it's every time at once!

How do we measure Earth time?

Lines of longitude start from the Prime Meridian (0°) and go east and west until they meet at 180°. **Greenwich Mean Time** (GMT) also starts out from 0°. Easterly places are always ahead of GMT and westerly places are behind.

How can it be every time at the poles?

The farthest points north and south on Earth are in all time zones. In theory, it is all times of the day here.*

* GMT is used at the North Pole.

WHERE IS THE SUNNIEST PLACE ON EARTH?

Yuma, Arizona, is officially the world's sunniest place, with 4,000 hours of sunshine a year.

How much sun is that per day?

With over 4,015 hours of sunlight out of a possible 4,500 hours of daylight, Yuma never has less than 8 hours of sunshine a day. That's a 90 percent chance of sunshine … every day!

Where can we find the sunniest month?

May on Ellesmere Island is the sunniest month of the year anywhere. This is one of the most northerly settlements on Earth, where in summer the Sun never drops below the horizon. This Canadian outpost averages about 16.5 hours of sunshine per day.

DOES LIGHTNING STRIKE TWICE?

The Willis Tower in Chicago gets struck by lightning up to 100 times a year!

What causes lightning?

Lightning is an electric current from the sky. Static electricity in clouds causes electrical charge to build up on the ground, often on the tallest object. When a connection is made, electricity flashes between the ground and the clouds.

How much energy does lightning have?

A single bolt of lightning contains enough energy to cook 100,000 pieces of toast.

Who is the biggest lightning survivor?

Roy Sullivan, a US park ranger, was hit by lightning seven times between 1942 and 1977. He survived every single strike.

WHERE IS THE WORLD'S HOTTEST PLACE?

Death Valley, USA. Walking through here during the day is not recommended.

What other record does Death Valley claim?

High temperatures are not the only unique thing about the largest national park in the USA outside Alaska. At 86 m (282 ft) below sea level, Badwater Basin is a low point—the USA's lowest in fact!

How hot does it get?

Death Valley, USA, holds the official record for the highest temperature: 57 °C (134 °F), measured on July 10, 1913.

How do plants survive here?

Thirsty plants in Death Valley shoot roots 30 m (100 ft) into the ground to slurp up whatever water they can find.

WHERE IS THE CHILLIEST PLACE ON EARTH?

In 2013, NASA satellites measured temperatures in Antarctica of -94.7 °C (-135.8 °F).

How can you breathe in freezing air?

It's no surprise that this frozen continent is the coldest place on Earth. Temperatures in Antarctica are so cold that scientists use a breathing tube that pipes air up their coatsleeves to warm it before they take it into their lungs.

What was the previous record?

Until the NASA measurements, the lowest recorded temperature was a bone-chilling -89.2 °C (-128.6 °F). This was measured on the ground at the Vostok Research Station.

Can you survive the cold without clothes?

Only for a short time. To stave off the boredom, Antarctic researchers dare each other to do naked sprints through the snow in toe-curling -73 °C (-100 °F) temperatures!

How strong were the icest winds?

In 1913, an Antarctic expedition stopped at Commonwealth Bay. In July, the winds here hit 153 km/h (95 mph). It's actually very hard to measure wind speed in the Antarctic, as when it really blows it tends to destroy the equipment!

What was the fastest gust recorded?

In 1996, an unmanned weather station on Barrow Island, Western Australia, recorded the strongest gust of wind ever, which tipped 408 km/h (253 mph).

Where can you find the most tornadoes?

Oklahoma's "Tornado Alley," in the USA's heartland, is the home of the twister. In April 2011, 207 tornadoes formed in a single day.

HOW MUCH OF EARTH'S SURFACE IS COVERED IN WATER?

Nearly three-quarters, 71 percent, of our planet's surface is flooded.

Where is Earth's water?

Our planet sloshes with liquid water. Almost all of it (about 96.5%) is salt water in the seas. Water also fills the sky as water vapor and clouds; runs in rivers and lakes; and is stored in ice caps, glaciers, and underground aquifers. Living things are, also, mostly made up of water.

Does the water stay put?

Water never stays still. The planet's water constantly moves from the sea to the sky, falling as rain that feeds rivers and fills aquifers. It changes from one form to another.

HOW MANY CELLS ARE IN A HUMAN BODY?

Your body contains countless microscopic building blocks, some say up to 100 trillion.

The membrane is like a bag around the cell.

What are cells?

All living things are made of **cells**. You need a microscope to see them. These tiny, self-contained units are surrounded by a membrane that acts like the walls of a house. It keeps unwanted things outside, while inside is a watery liquid that contains all the chemicals needed to make the body work.

How big is a trillion?

A trillion is a million million, or 1 followed by 12 zeros. If you counted non-stop from one to a trillion, at a rate of one number every second, it would take you about 32,000 years!

There are more living things on your skin than there are humans living on the planet.

ARE WE FULL OF BACTERIA?

You carry around almost ten times more bacterial cells than your own body cells.

Is our bacteria harmful?

Most of the cells in your body don't actually belong to you! But don't worry—bacteria actually keep you healthy. In fact, without all these alien germs, you probably wouldn't last long. Most of them live inside your guts and are very useful. They help you to break down the food you eat.

How heavy are our microbes?

All these extra microbes weigh as much as 1.4 kg (3 lbs).

HOW LONG IS HUMAN DNA?

The human body carries enough DNA to stretch from Earth to Pluto 17 times!

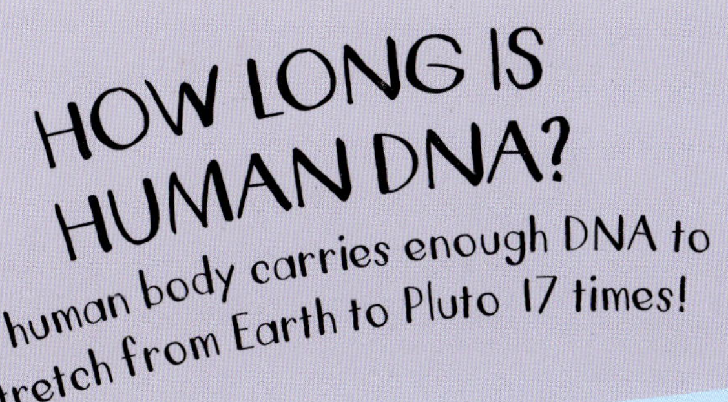

Just how much DNA is that?

There are 6 billion km (3.7 billion miles) between Earth and Pluto. Going at speeds of up to 83,000 km/h (51,000 mph), it took NASA's New Horizons spacecraft 10 years to reach Pluto. If it went at that speed along your DNA, it would take 323 years to reach the end.

How long is DNA?

Every cell of your body contains tightly coiled DNA inside its nucleus. If you unwound the DNA in one cell, it would stretch a staggering 2 m (6 ft). Don't try this at home!

ARE HUMANS MOSTLY WATER?

Your body is sloshing with liquid.

Where is our body's water?

You are a giant bag of water! Or, more precisely, like lots of tiny bags of water, because most of the liquid in your body is found inside cells. Each of the 100 trillion cells in your body is about two-thirds water.

How much of a baby is water?

A newborn is about three-quarters water.

Where's the rest of the water?

An average-sized body has about 14 l (4 gallons) of water outside its cells. This includes the liquid part of blood, the fluid surrounding the brain and spinal cord, the liquid of the eyes, joint lubricant, and lymph— a watery liquid surrounding cells.

HOW MUCH BLOOD DO WE CARRY?

Adults have about 5 l (11 pints) of blood.

How many red blood cells do we have?

About a quarter of the cells in your body are red blood cells.

Why do blood veins look blue?

Blood is never blue. Your veins look blue because only blue light penetrates the skin deep enough to be reflected by the veins.

What does blood do?

Blood carries oxygen and nutrients to your body cells and takes away waste.

How far do blood cells travel?

A red blood cell makes a complete circuit of your body in just a minute.

Does all blood look the same?

Oxygen-carrying blood in arteries is bright red; blood not carrying oxygen in veins appears darker.

The liquid part of your blood, called **plasma**, is actually yellow!

How many cells are in a drop of blood?

One drop of blood contains about 250 million oxygen-carrying red blood cells.

Do we make new blood cells?

Your body makes 2 million new blood cells every second.

HOW MUCH IRON IS IN OUR BODIES?

Most people have about 4.5 g (0.16 oz) of iron in their bodies, enough to make a 7- cm (3- in) nail.

Where is all this iron?

About half of the iron inside your body is found in your blood, where it is used to carry oxygen to your cells. The rest is dotted around in places such as the liver, spleen, and bone marrow.

How much calcium do we have?

As well as iron, you also contain about 1 kg (2.2 lbs) of calcium in your bones and teeth. That's enough to make more than 18,000 sticks of chalk.

HOW LARGE ARE LUNGS?

Stretched out flat, your lungs could cover a tennis court. They keep you supplied with oxygen and get rid of waste gases that builds up in the body.

How big is a tennis court?

A tennis court measures 23 × 11 m (78 × 36 ft).

What are lungs for?

Your lungs' job is getting gas into and out of your bloodstream. They maximize the contact area between your blood and the air. Inside each lung are 300 million tiny air sacs, called alveoli, each covered by a network of small blood vessels.

Are lungs equal sized?

Your left lung is a little smaller than your right. This is to leave room in the chest cavity for your heart.

DO BABIES HAVE MORE BONES THAN ADULTS?

Adults have 206 bones in their bodies. Babies have 270. So how come babies' bodies are so wonderfully soft?

Why do babies have funny-shaped heads?

A newborn baby's skull bones are not yet fused together. Cartilage between the bones allows the skull to squish.

Why do babies have more bones?

Babies must travel down a narrow birth canal to be born. To make the journey easier, many bones start out in pieces, joined by bendy cartilage. Later, this cartilage hardens into bone.

WHERE IS THE SMALLEST BONE IN THE BODY?

Listen up! The smallest bones are inside your ear.

The stapes bone looks like a riding stirrup. It measures about 3 × 2.5 mm (0.12 × 0.1 in).

How do we hear?

Your ear has an unusual and elaborate mechanism to carry vibrations in the air to your brain. The flappy outer part of your ear channels sounds down your earhole, where the air beats on the thin skin of the eardrum.

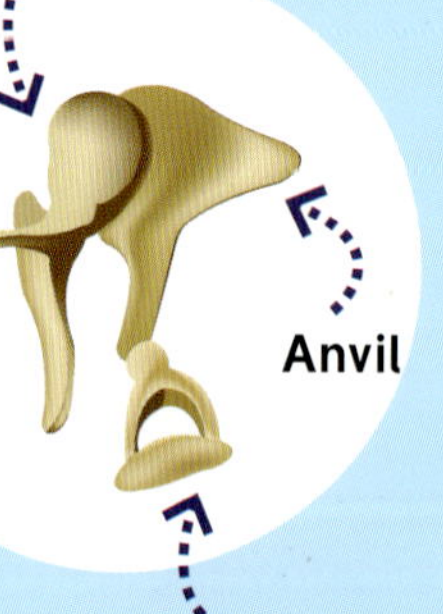

What's behind the eardrum?

Behind the eardrum, in your middle ear, three tiny bones transmit vibrations to the inner ear. Here, the shaking movements are turned into nerve impulses that get sent to your brain.

ARE BABIES EVER BORN WITH TEETH?

Most babies are just born with gums, but on rare occasions they arrive with a tiny tooth as well.

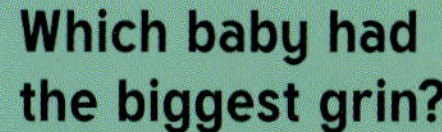

Which baby had the biggest grin?

The record for the most teeth at birth belongs to Sean Keaney of Newbury, UK. He was born with 12 teeth.

When do most babies get their teeth?

Usually, babies don't get their first tooth until they are about six months old. But some lucky parents get a shock when their newborn smiles at them … and shows a shiny white tooth! Only about one in every 2,000 babies is born with a tooth.

How tough is tooth enamel?

Tooth enamel is the hardest material in the body.

HOW MANY SETS OF TEETH DO WE GROW?

Just two, milk teeth as babies then adult teeth meant to last us into old age.

I. BABY BITES

Babies grow milk teeth between four and seven months of age. By three years old, most kids have a full set of 20 baby teeth.

2. BIG BITERS

When you reach about five or six years old, your milk teeth start to fall out, making way for a total of 32 adult teeth. This is your final set of teeth, so take care of them!

3. OLDER AND WISER?

The last four adult teeth grow later than the rest. Wisdom teeth usually arrive between the ages of 17 and 21.

HOW MANY MUSCLES DO WE HAVE?

The human body has 650 muscles. These are the densest, heaviest parts of your body.

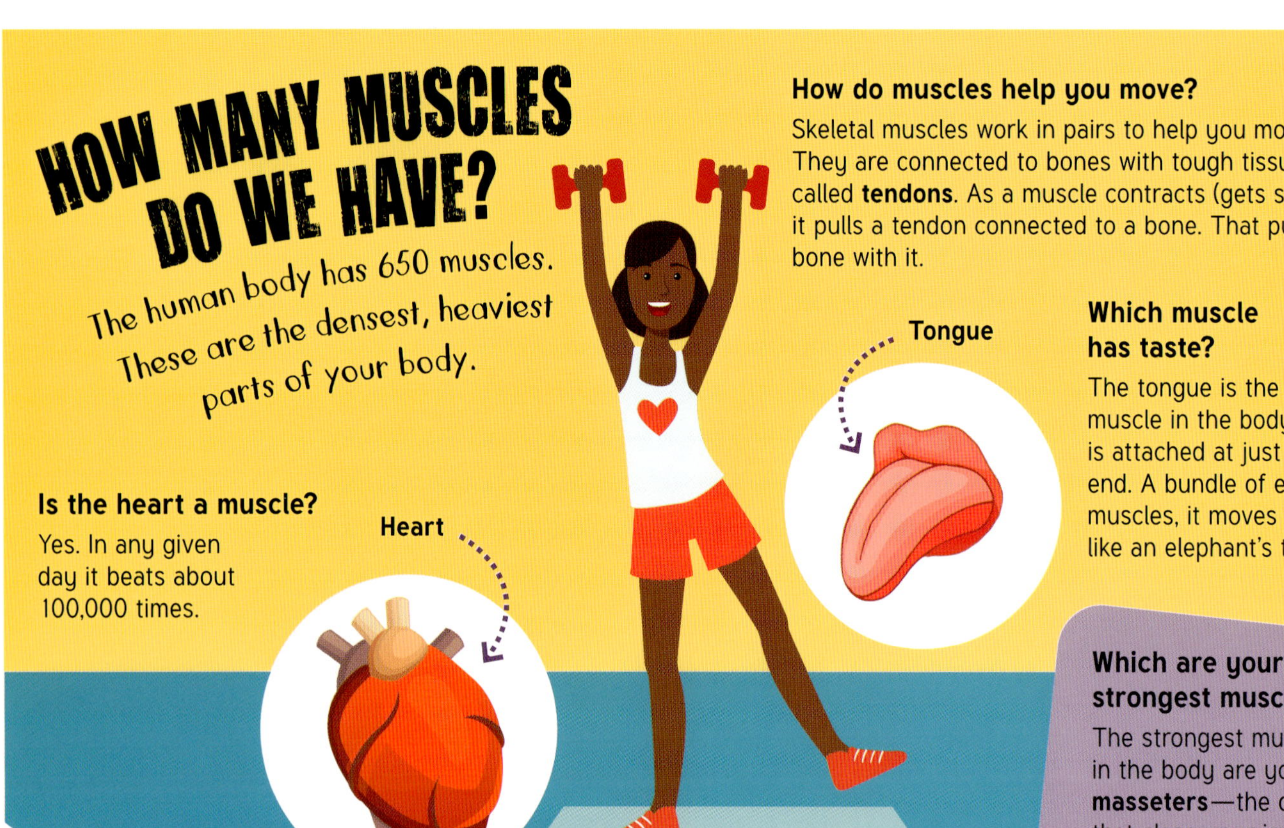

Is the heart a muscle?

Yes. In any given day it beats about 100,000 times.

How do muscles help you move?

Skeletal muscles work in pairs to help you move. They are connected to bones with tough tissues called **tendons**. As a muscle contracts (gets smaller), it pulls a tendon connected to a bone. That pulls the bone with it.

Which muscle has taste?

The tongue is the only muscle in the body that is attached at just one end. A bundle of eight muscles, it moves flexibly like an elephant's trunk.

Which are your strongest muscles?

The strongest muscles in the body are your **masseters**—the ones that close your jaws.

What is your biggest organ?

Covering the entire body, **skin** is your largest organ. As well as containing your insides in a nice, flexible package, it protects you from bumps and bruises, and keeps out infectious bugs. Skin also plays a crucial role in keeping you cool.

WHERE IS THE BODY'S LARGEST ORGAN?

Some people think the largest organ is the liver, but it's not, it's your skin!

How heavy is skin?

An adult's **skin** weighs around 3.6 kg (8 lbs).

How often do you swap skin?

Cells in the skin's base layer constantly divide to make new copies of themselves. As old skin cells flake off, they move to the surface. Your skin replaces itself about every month.

HOW DO YOU DIGEST?

Your digestive system breaks down food and drink into parts it can use, and gets rid of the waste.

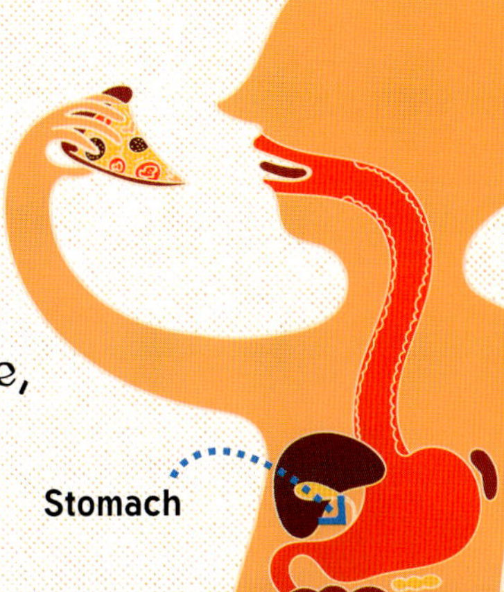

How much saliva do you produce?

Breaking down food begins in the mouth with chewing and saliva. You make more than 1 l (2 pints) of saliva every day.

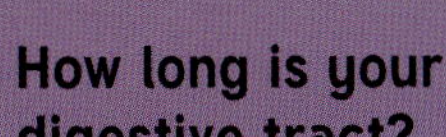

How long is your digestive tract?

Your **digestive tract** is a tube that runs from your mouth to your bottom. It is about 10 m (33 ft) long—almost as long as a school bus.

What is the small intestine for?

The small intestine absorbs most of the nutrients from food. Water is recovered in the large intestine, before the waste leaves your body.

Your guts are divided into small and large intestines.

The surface area of your small intestine is about ten times greater than that of your skin.

What causes farting?

Your guts are also packed with bacteria. The gases they release make you fart.

How long does a meal stay in your body?

It normally takes six-to-eight hours for a meal to pass through your body.

Chemicals made by the liver, pancreas, and gall bladder turn food and drink into nutrients that the body can use as fuel.

How long was the longest belch?

In 2009, Michele Forgione produced a record-breaking belch in Reggiolo, Italy. His epic tummy rumble lasted 1 minute, 13 seconds!

DO BUGS LIVE ON YOUR FACE?

Your eyelashes and eyebrows are home to eight-legged micro-mites.

Demodex

Which mite might live in your hair?

Meet **Demodex**. This critter lives on your head. Measuring 0.3 mm (0.01 in) long, it looks like a tiny finger with short, stubby legs at one end. Demodex mites are harmless and bury themselves head-down in hair follicles, peacefully eating the oils we secrete. At night, they come up to crawl around on the surface and meet other mites.

Does everyone get these mites?

Sorry. Recent studies have shown that 100% of adults have mite DNA on their faces!

WHAT'S LIVING INSIDE YOUR PILLOW?

How much skin do you lose?

Tough old skin cells at the surface of your skin flake off all the time. In just one minute, about 30,000–40,000 skin cells fall off your body. That adds up to about 4 kg (9 lbs) of dead skin cells shed every year—the same as a bag of barbecue coals.

What makes up the weight of a pillow?

After two years, scientists calculate that a third of the weight of your pillow is made up of germs, dust mites, dust mite poop, and dead skin cells. Sweet dreams!

Dust mite

HOW HEAVY IS YOUR BRAIN?

The brain accounts for just one-fiftieth of your bodyweight, but it gobbles up a fifth of the energy.

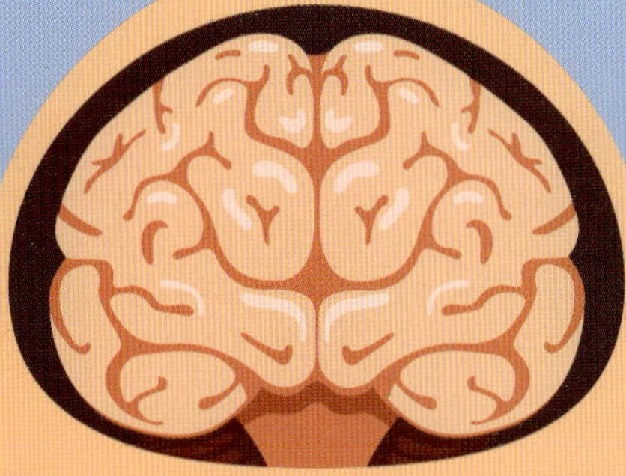

What does a brain feel like?

Your brain has roughly the same texture as soft tofu.

How does a human brain compare to animal brains?

The human brain is over three times as large as the brains of other mammals of equal body size.

Why is the brain wrinkly?

The outer surface of the brain is wrinkled and folded up to squeeze lots of grey matter into the tight space under your skull.

Does the brain make energy?

Your brain buzzes with electricity, and produces enough to power a 12-watt lightbulb.

Can the brain feel?

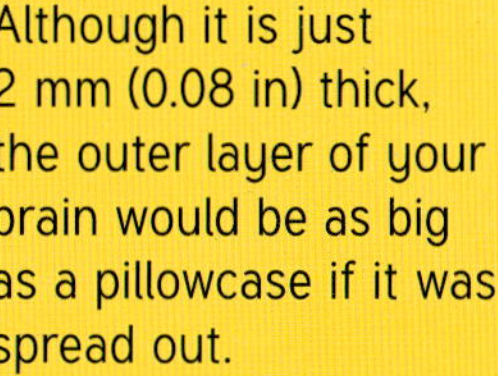

The brain has no nerve endings of its own. This means it cannot sense when it is in pain—special pain receptors have to tell it.

How long are the brain's nerves?

If you untangled the billions of extremely thin nerve fibers in the brain, they would wrap around the planet four times.

How many connections are in the brain?

Your brain contains about 200 trillion connections. That's about 1,000 times the number of stars in the Milky Way.

What's special about your brain?

You are the only person in the entire world with your exact set of brain connections. This makes you unique.

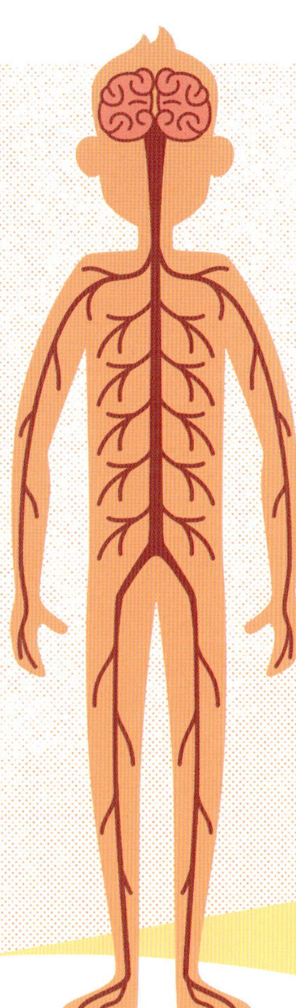

What job do nerves do?

Your nerves constantly carry electrical and chemical signals, zapping messages around your body. They provide your brain with information on the outside world and the state of your insides. They also control your muscles and essential body processes.

Where are you most sensitive?

The most sensitive bits of your body are where nerve endings cluster together. A thumbnail-sized patch of skin contains around 50 nerve endings.

WHY DO YOU FEEL SO NERVOUS?

You have nearly 75 km (46 miles) of nerves in your body.

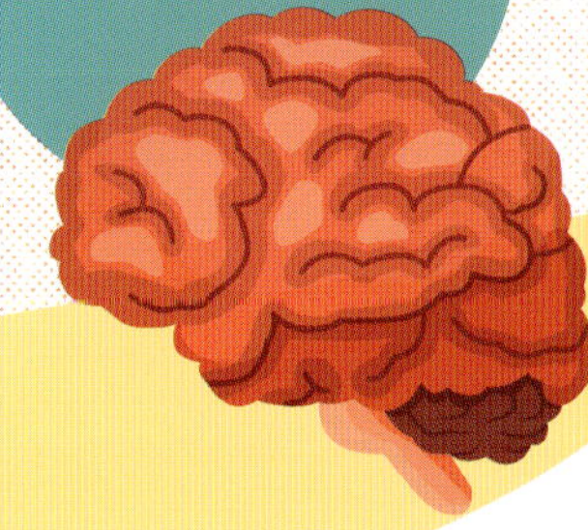

The brain contains about 100 billion microscopic nerve cells.

HOW FAST DO NERVE SIGNALS TRAVEL?

Faster than a race car. Your body certainly knows how to deliver a message!

How fast is fast?

Nerves operate at different speeds. Your fastest nerve fibers transmit messages at about 400 km/h (250 mph)—faster than the speediest racing car.

What makes nerve signals so fast?

Your fastest nerve fibers carry reflexes. They are coated in a fat called myelin and can transmit signals 20 times quicker than other nerves. They carry pressure and pain signals so you automatically move away from harm.

Are babies up to speed?

By the time you are four years old, your nerves are at full speed. Newborn and toddler nerves run at about half speed.

HOW TASTY IS YOUR TONGUE?

You have about 10,000 taste buds on your tongue. Most are on the tip.

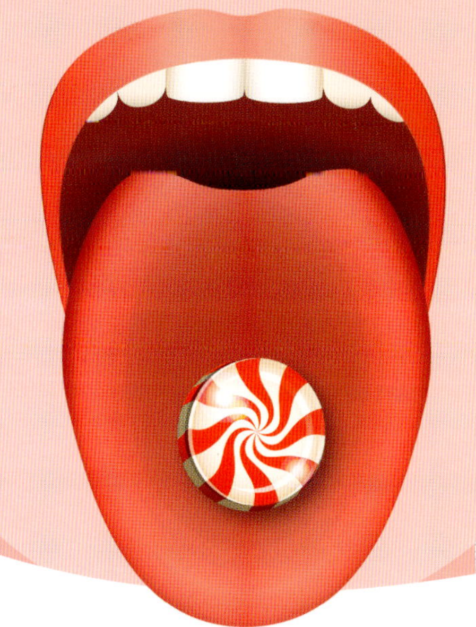

How do you taste?

Tiny taste buds, invisible to the human eye, cluster around the small bumps on your tongue. Each bud has around 50 to 150 taste-receptor cells, which send taste nerve signals to your brain.

You can sense just five basic tastes— bitter, sweet, salty, sour, and umami (a meaty flavor).

How long can tongues get?

Californian Nick Stoeberl is the proud owner of the world's longest tongue. His title-winning tongue measures 10.1 cm (3.97 in) from its tip to the middle of the closed top lip.

Do you have taste buds elsewhere?

There are taste buds on the roof of your mouth, in your throat, your gullet, and even inside your guts.

Why do bugs like your mouth?

Your mouth is heavenly for bacteria. There's yummy, sugary food aplenty, no shortage of water, and a constant temperature of 36.5 °C (97.7 °F).

HOW MANY BUGS ARE IN YOUR MOUTH?

There are more bugs in your mouth than there are people on Earth!

Are all mouth bugs the same?

A person might have as many as 200-300 different species of microbe in their mouth. In all, scientists have identified more than 615 different types of bacteria in people's mouths.

How many bugs are in one drop of saliva?

Just one drop of saliva has over 100 million micro-bugs. Depending on the individual—and how often they brush their teeth—there could be anywhere between 100,000 and 1 billion bacteria living on each tooth.

HOW MANY BABIES ARE BORN EACH SECOND?

Four babies are born every second somewhere in the world.

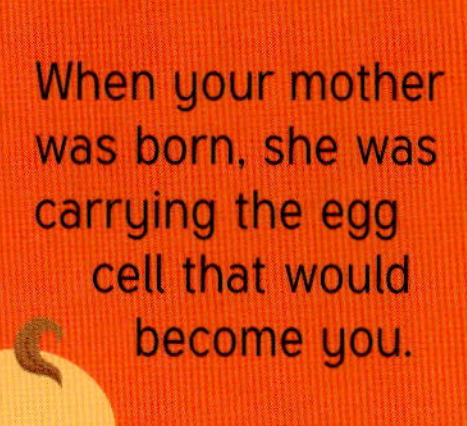

Does your brain keep on growing?

By the time you are six years old, your brain is nearly fully grown.

Do babies grow faster than adults?

Yes. If you kept growing at the rate of your first year, by the age of 20 you'd be a 7.5- m (24.5- ft) giant who weighed 140 kg (309 lbs)!

Can babies cry?

Babies can make noise but they can't shed tears until they are at least a month old.

Why do you get pimples?

As you become an adult, your skin produces more oil, so you get more pimples.

Are babies smarter?

Babies' brains have more connections than adult brains.

Do old people shrink?

The wearing down of protective cartilage pads in leg joints and between spine bones can knock 5 cm (2 in) off your height by the age of 70.

IS EVERYTHING MADE OF ATOMS?

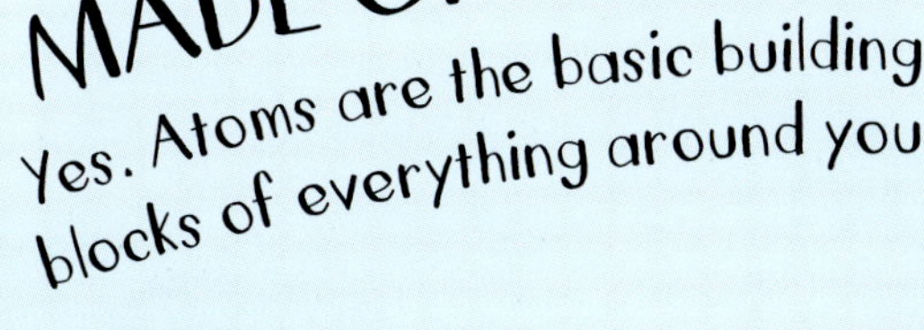

Yes. Atoms are the basic building blocks of everything around you.

What are atoms?

Atoms are tiny particles of matter. Invisible to all but the most powerful electron microscopes, these tiny units are always jiggling and moving about. They join together in unimaginably vast numbers to build all the big stuff of our world.

Who "invented" atoms?

Ancient Greek philosopher Democritus came up with the idea of atoms. However, they weren't discovered until the 20th century.

How many atoms do you have?

There are something like 7 million billion trillion atoms in the human body.

ARE ATOMS MOSTLY EMPTY SPACE?

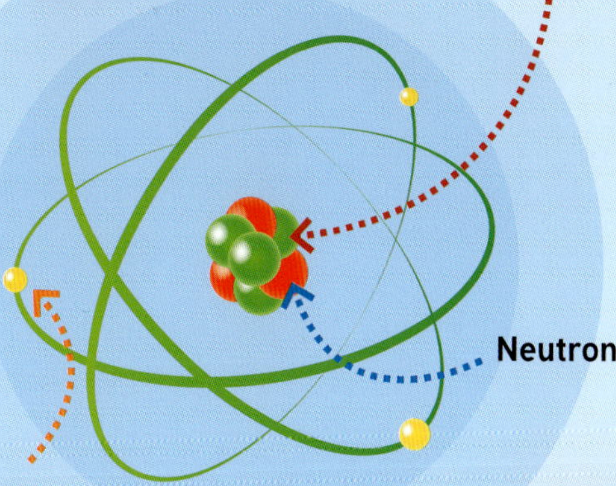

What are atoms made of?

Atoms are made of three different kinds of minuscule particles—positively charged protons, neutral neutrons, and negatively charged electrons. The protons and the neutrons stick together extremely tightly in the atom's core. Powerfully attracted to this positive nucleus, the electrons orbit around it. Even though this picture isn't 100 percent accurate, it's a useful way to imagine an atom.

The number of protons decides what type of atom, or "element" it is.

The number of protons and electrons is usually balanced, so that an atom has no overall charge.

Where is most of an atom?

The majority of an atom's mass is in the nucleus.

HOW MANY ELEMENTS ARE THERE?

There are 118 types of atom, called "elements."

What are the most common elements?

Together, the elements hydrogen and helium make up 98 percent of the matter in the universe.

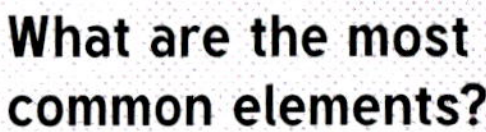

The Sun burns up 620 million tonnes (683 million tons) of hydrogen every second.

What is the rarest natural element?

Astatine is the rarest element found in nature—just 30 g (1 oz) of it exists in the Earth's crust at any time.

The heavy metals **osmium** and **iridium** are twice as heavy as lead!

The most reactive elements are **fluorine** and **francium**.

What is the most expensive element?

At $27 million per gram, **californium** is the most expensive element.

How many elements occur naturally?

Just 92 elements occur naturally on Earth.

Which metal is a liquid at room temperature?

The element **mercury** is the only metal that is liquid at room temperature.

How old is hydrogen?

Hydrogen atoms were made during the Big Bang—this makes them an awesome 13.8 billion years old!

What's special about metals?

Metals are mostly shiny materials, which reflect light. They are generally amazing at conducting heat and electricity. This is because of the way atoms join together in metals. The outer electrons of each atom are free to drift through the material. This also makes metals very tough, but flexible.

HOW MUCH MATTER IS METALLIC?

A quirk of matter is that more than three quarters of it is metallic.

How much iron is in Earth's core?

Earth's core contains enough iron to make a train rail that would loop the globe 50 billion times.

Copper and **gold** are strange, because, unlike other metals, they are not silvery.

HOW MUCH GOLD HAS BEEN MINED?

All the gold ever mined would fit into a surprisingly small cube.*

Where is most of the gold?

Bright and lustrous, gold is the must-have metal that people go crazy for. Because it is virtually indestructible, all the gold that has been dug out of the ground is still with us—although most of it is locked in bank vaults.

Who has the most gold?

The biggest amount of gold found in one place is 550,000 gold bars, stored deep beneath the subway in the vault of the Federal Reserve Bank of New York. It's worth over $200 billion.

*A cube with sides of 20 m (67 ft).

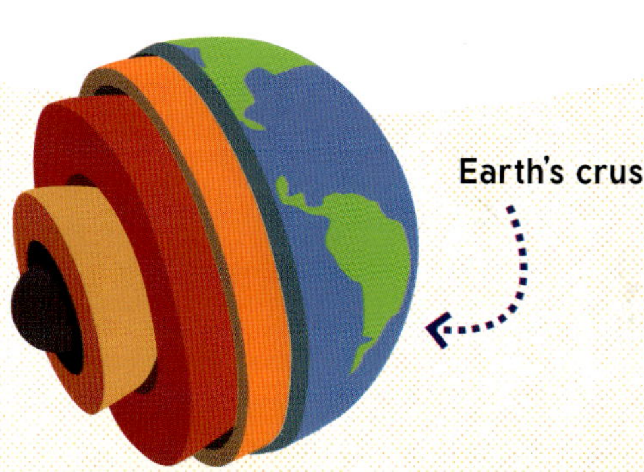

WHAT'S SO GREAT ABOUT CARBON?

Carbon is the fourth most common element and the most versatile.

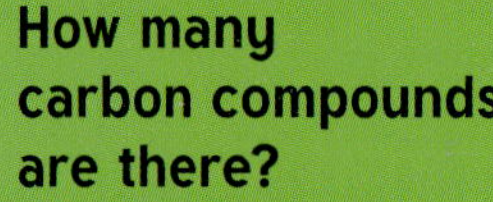

Can carbon be combined?

Carbon is great at combining with other elements (and with itself, too). It forms a vast number of substances. Plastics and petroleum products are all carbon compounds! Carbon is added to steel to make it hard, and to resin to make super-light, super-strong, carbon-fiber composites.

Are you part carbon?

All life we know about, from tiny microbes to giant whales, uses carbon-based chemistry. Our bodies rely on molecules built around chains of carbon.

DO PENCILS CONTAIN LEAD?

Pencil leads have nothing to do with lead. They are made from a form of carbon called **graphite**.

What is made from carbon?

All atoms of the same element have exactly the same number of protons. But that doesn't mean they always link together in the same way. Carbon forms crystal-clear and super-hard diamonds—the hardest substance found in nature—deep under Earth's surface. It also forms dark, soft, and slippery graphite. This greasy form of carbon is the one used in pencils.

HOW LONG DOES NUCLEAR WASTE STAY DANGEROUS?

Nuclear waste remains deadly for a quarter of a million years.

Is nuclear energy clean?

Nuclear power stations use long rods of radioactive uranium-238 as fuel. Using powerful nuclear reactions, they produce "clean" electricity. Unlike fossil-fuel-burning power stations, they produce no carbon dioxide. There is one major problem, though. Their spent fuel is highly radioactive.

How is nuclear waste stored?

A large reactor produces 20–30 tonnes (22–33 tons) of waste per year. It's dangerously radioactive. High-level waste is kept in storage pools for 20 years. Then it is packed into strong barrels and buried under the ground.

Should you avoid bananas?

Doctors calculate that you would need to eat 10,000,000 bananas in one sitting to die of radiation poisoning, or 274 bananas a day for seven years to notice any effect. Eating bananas isn't going to turn you into a mutant supervillain in a hurry.

ARE BANANAS RADIOACTIVE?

Yes! Bananas contain lots of potassium, which can be radioactive ...

How radioactive are bananas?

Not all potassium atoms are radioactive, just those with 19 protons and 21 neutrons—called K-40. Luckily, only a tiny 0.012% of potassium is dangerous K-40. Each banana contains a miniscule 0.000001 oz (0.0000393 g) ot K-40.

WHY DOES ICE FLOAT?

Water expands when it freezes. This is why ice floats in water.

What makes freezing water expand?

Most liquids shrink when they freeze and turn into a solid. Not water. Ice crystals have a more open arrangement of molecules compared to liquid water. As they grow in freezing water, they push outward, expanding the volume by nearly ten percent.

How big can icebergs get?

The world's largest iceberg measured 295 km (183 miles) long and 37 km (23 miles) wide, larger than the island of Jamaica.

WHY IS CHEMISTRY IMPORTANT?

Most things around us are not made of single elements. Chemistry is all about how different atoms and molecules interact with each other.

How are molecules made?

Atoms join together to make molecules, either by sharing electrons or by taking electrons from each other.

What is a chemical reaction?

A chemical reaction happens when one substance changes into another. Sometimes this is irreversible—when you bake a cake, there's no way to reverse the reaction to get back to the raw ingredients. Other reactions can go both ways, from starting materials to products, and back again.

WHY IS OXYGEN AWESOME?

One in five parts of Earth's atmosphere is made up of oxygen.

The gas we breathe is made of two atoms of oxygen joined together—O_2.

Is ozone oxygen?

Ozone is made of three atoms of oxygen joined together—O_3.

Oxygen is the most common element on our planet's surface.

High up in the atmosphere a layer of ozone gas protects us from the Sun's damaging UV, or ultraviolet, radiation.

How does oxygen help life?

Oxygen powers the chemical reactions that keep life going on Earth.

How common is oxygen?

After hydrogen and helium, **oxygen** is the third most common element in the Universe.

Oxygen is so reactive that on Earth it is always found combined with other elements.

Can we breathe pure oxygen?

Breathing pure oxygen for more than 16 hours is fatal.

What does oxygen look like?

Oxygen gas is transparent; liquid oxygen is blue.

Around 300 million years ago, there was so much oxygen in the air that wildfires would have burned even wet plants.

WHY WAS THOMAS MIDGELEY JR. THE WORLD'S MOST DANGEROUS SCIENTIST?

This well-meaning scientist invented the most dangerous chemicals in history.

How did Midgeley damage the atmosphere?

Midgeley threatened the planet with **chlorofluorocarbons** (CFCs). Although safer than other chemicals used in refrigerators at the time, these gases destroy ozone high in the atmosphere. In 1985, scientists discovered a huge hole in the ozone layer that protects Earth from the Sun's UV rays.

How did Midgeley damage brains?

In the 1920s, Midgeley pioneered adding lead to gasoline. This made car engines run more smoothly and improved their mileage. Unfortunately, the lead-laced fumes were toxic and damaging to brains. Leaded gas was finally banned in the 1990s.

WHAT CHEMICAL LIFESAVER GROWS ON MOLDY BREAD?

Penicillin may well have saved your life. Without it, sore throats and infected cuts can sometimes become fatal.

How was pencillin discovered?

Scottish chemist Alexander Fleming discovered the wonder drug penicillin by accident in 1928. He went on vacation without cleaning his petri dishes. When he returned, he noticed that the mold now growing on these dishes had stopped bacteria in its tracks!

Although he discovered penicillin, Fleming never actually found a good way to extract it. Pals Howard Florey and Ernest Chain finally figured out a way to purify penicillin in 1939.

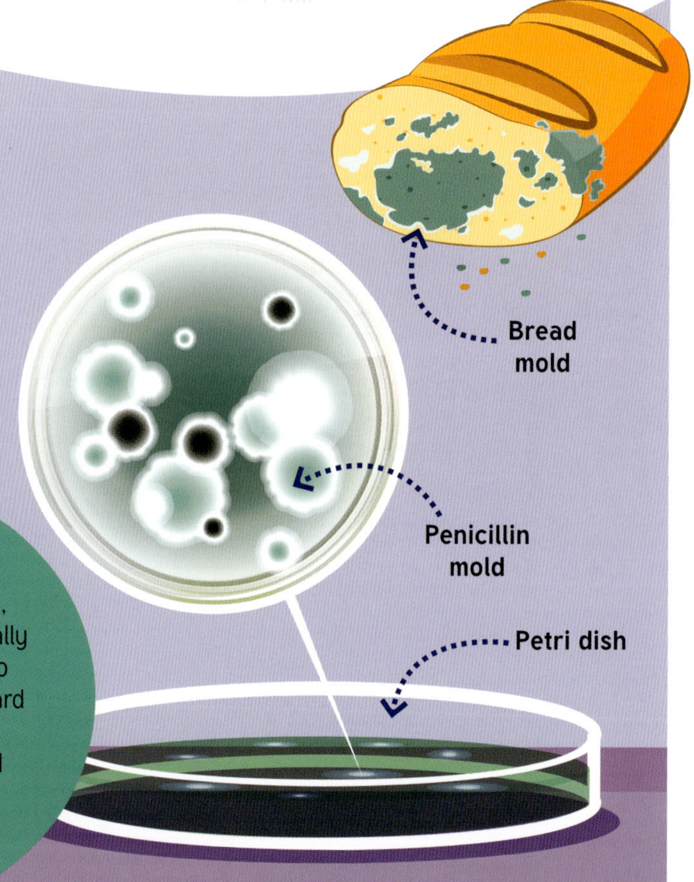

What was surgery like before antiseptics?

Before chemical antiseptics, surgery was very risky. Cuts could easily become infected by bacteria. These invisible microbes caused "ward fever." Even a patient who had a successful operation could later die from the infection.

Did surgeons keep clean?

Before the 1860s, surgeons wore filthy aprons and didn't sterilize their surgical instruments. They didn't always wash their hands before operating, either.

WHEN WAS ANTISEPTIC FIRST USED?

The first antiseptic was used in 1865 by Joseph Lister.

What did Joseph Lister introduce?

Lister covered wounds with dressings soaked in carbolic acid. He also introduced hand-washing, sterilizing instruments, and disinfecting with carbolic spray while operating. The rate of infection plummeted.

DID AN ANCIENT CIVILIZATION INVENT ELECTRICAL POWER?

The first battery was invented 2,000 years ago.

What was the first battery?

About 200 BCE, in what is now Iraq, a smart inventor built a very special clay pot. Inside was an iron bar, around which was a copper cylinder. This apparatus was bathed in acid and closed with a tar stopper. What this Mesopotamian "battery" was used for is still a mystery.

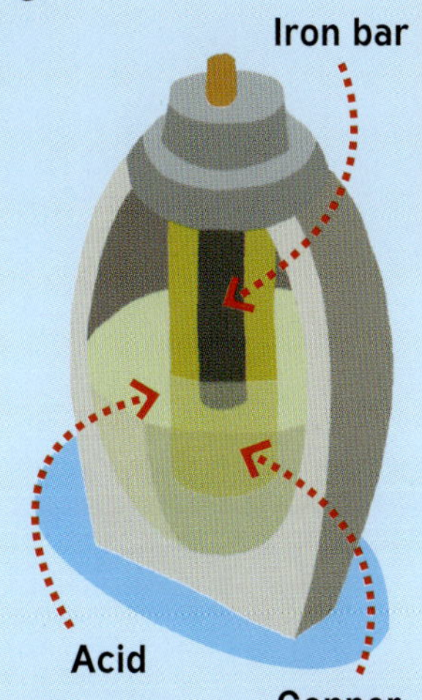

Who invented the modern battery?

Italian scientist Alessandro Volta invented the first modern battery in 1800. This high-tech sandwich of metal disks soaked in saltwater was the first reliable source of electrical energy.

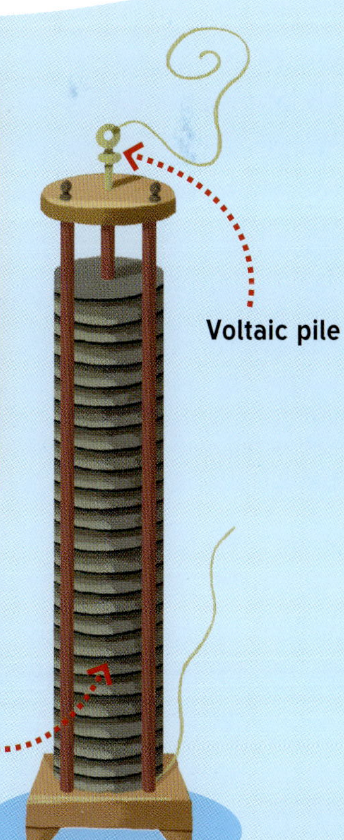

HOW PURE IS MICROCHIP SILICON?

The silicon in computer chips has to be ultra-pure to work.

How is silicon purified?

Only the purest silicon—electronic grade silicon—can be used to make silicon chips. The start of the process is making one enormous crystal of silicon, taller than an adult and weighing hundreds of kilos (or pounds). This is then purified, at temperatures hotter than molten lava (1,500 °C/2,700 °F).

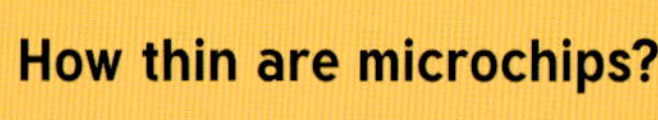

How thin are microchips?

Microchips are engraved into silicon wafers. Each wafer is cut to 0.5 mm (0.04 in) thick—about the width of a pencil lead, and then polished flatter-than-flat.

"Nine nines" purity = 99.9999999% pure!

What's so special about graphene?

Discovered in 2004, **graphene** is an ultralight, super-flexible material made of a net of carbon atoms arranged in hexagons, just like a honeycomb. In sheets a mere one-atom thick, graphene is transparent, and is the world's best conductor of electricity.

How strong is graphene?

Graphene is 200 times stronger than steel

WHAT IS THE WORLD'S THINNEST MATERIAL?

Graphene is the world's first 2D material, a million times thinner than a human hair.

How was graphene discovered?

Graphene was discovered by researchers cleaning graphite samples with tape. Checking the tape, the scientists realized that, along with the dust and dirt, they were ripping off super-thin graphene sheets.

WHAT IS CONCRETE MADE OF?

Concrete is made of sand and gravel, held together with lime cement.

Does concrete weaken?

Concrete gets stronger as it gets older.

When mixed with water, a chemical reaction occurs. Crystals grow, setting the concrete hard.

Who invented concrete?

The Romans invented modern concrete.

The Pantheon in Rome is the world's largest unreinforced concrete dome.

When was concrete invented?

The oldest known concrete is about 2,500 years old.

There are around 150 billion grains in 450 g (1 lb) of concrete.

The largest continuous concrete pour was enough to fill eight Olympic-sized swimming pools and took four days in 2017, in Sharjah, UAE.

Every 1 tonne (1.1 tons) of cement made produces 1 tonne (1.1 tons) of carbon dioxide.

Where is the world's largest concrete structure?

China's Three Gorges Dam is the world's largest, built with 16 million m³ (565 million ft³) of concrete!

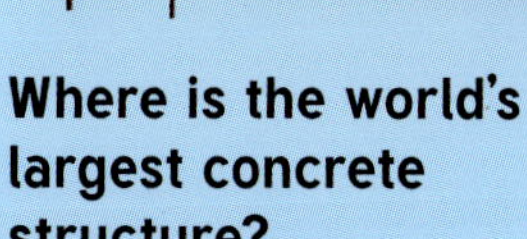

The Chinese added sticky rice to their concrete mixes when building the Great Wall of China.

Sticky rice

WHAT IS THE WORLD'S STRONGEST MATERIAL?

Another carbon wonder material, carbyne, is EVEN stronger than graphene.

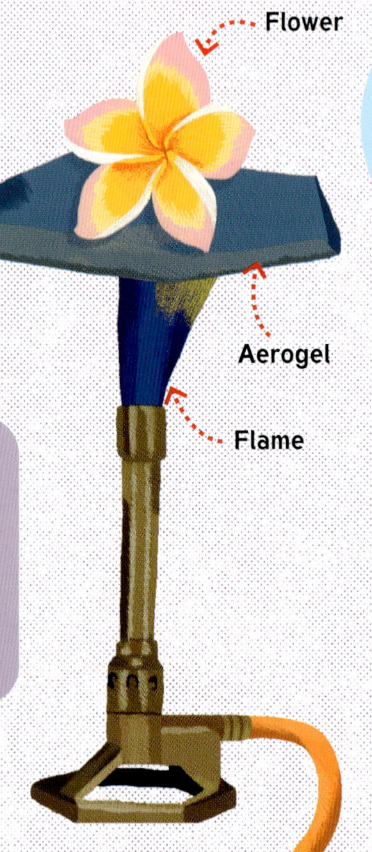

What is carbyne?

Carbyne is made of long chains of carbon just one-atom wide and invisible to the naked eye. Although predicted over 50 years ago, researchers have only recently learned how to make the molecule. In 2014, they joined together a record 6,400 carbon atoms.

Can carbyne be found in nature?

Although it's tricky to make carbyne on Earth, it has been spotted in space. These carbon chains exist on asteroids and in clouds of interstellar dust.

WHAT ARE THE WORLD'S LIGHTEST SUBSTANCES?

Aerogels are a class of materials that are mostly made of air.

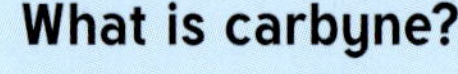

Around 99.98% of the volume of aerogels is air.

How are aerogels made?

These lightweight substances, nicknamed "solid smoke," start out life as a gel. They are then dried in a pressure vessel, which leaves the solid part intact, but riddled with microscopic holes where the liquid was. Aerogels are completely dry to touch.

What are aerogels used for?

Because they have such a large surface area, aerogels are amazing at mopping up spills. They are also good insulators, meaning that they can protect something as delicate as a flower from a naked flame.

HOW MUCH TIME DO YOU SPEND WATCHING TV?

It's fun to watch TV, but it can be a huge waste of time!

How does the time add up?

If, like the average person, you spend three and a half hours a day watching TV, that amounts to more than four days every month spent gazing at the screen. A month and a half of TV time every year! Just remember there's something called "outside," and that occasionally you may want to go out and see the world for yourself!

Where is the most TV watched?

Indonesia leads the world in screen time.

The average American watches about five hours of TV a day.

Are radio waves just for radio?

Radio waves are great for communication. They are used to broadcast TV and radio shows around the world, but they can also bounce telephone chat and Internet traffic around the planet via satellites. Radio signals even help us to communicate with space probes on distant planets.

WHAT ARE RADIO WAVES?

Radio waves are a form of electromagnetic energy that crosses vast distances.

How low can you go?

Submarines use very low frequency (VLF) and extremely low frequency (ELF) radio waves, which can travel through water to communicate with the surface.

Does Wi-Fi use radio waves?

Wi-Fi, Bluetooth, and wireless transmissions use extremely high frequency (EHF) radio waves.

IS ARCHITECTURE A SPORT?

Architecture was one of the five arts-oriented events (e.g., music, painting) at the Olympic Games until 1948. Medals were first awarded at the 1912 Summer Olympics in Stockholm, Sweden.

How deep is the Shard?

The Shard in London is western Europe's tallest building. Its foundations plunge 53 m (174 ft) deep underground, too.

Sidu River Bridge in China has the longest drop from the bridge deck to the ground, with a height of 496 m (1,627 ft).

How long is the Channel Tunnel?

The 50.45- km (31.3- mile) long Channel Tunnel between France and England has the longest undersea stretch of 37.9 km (23.5 miles).

How tall can you build?

When completed in 2029, the Jeddah Tower in Saudi Arabia will be the first building to reach 1 km (0.6 miles) high.

Which building is a master of disguise?

Clad with 33,000 extremely thin titanium sheets, the Guggenheim Museum in Bilbao looks like a flower from above and a ship from ground level.

About 1,000 elephants helped build the **Taj Mahal**, the world's most elaborate tomb.

What is the world's largest steel structure?

Beijing's "Bird's Nest" stadium is made of 36 km (22 miles) of unwrapped steel weighing 110,000 tonnes (121,254 tons).

The Roman aqueduct, **Pont du Gard**, was made without mortar. Its 5.4- tonne (6- ton) stone blocks fit perfectly together.

The Great Mosque of Djenné in Mali is the world's largest mud-brick structure.

WHAT IS THE WORLD'S TALLEST BUILDING?

The Burj Khalifa is three times taller than the Eiffel Tower and nearly twice as tall as the Empire State Building.

Nearly a kilometer high, at 828 m (2,716.5 ft) tall, the **Burj Khalifa** in Dubai, United Arab Emirates (UAE), is the tallest freestanding structure in the world.

No fewer than five of the largest passenger planes could be built with the aluminum used on the skyscraper.

What other records does it hold?

The Burj Khalifa has the world's longest elevator, ascending 140 floors.

How much concrete was used?

The concrete used to build the tower weighs the same as 100,000 elephants.

WHERE IS THE WORLD'S LARGEST ARTIFICIAL ISLAND?

The Palm Jumeirah was built off the coast of Dubai.

How big is the Palm Jumeirah?

The **Palm Jumeirah** is a weird and wonderful engineering marvel. It is an artificial island in the sea off Dubai, UAE. It covers an area greater than 800 soccer fields. But even more surprisingly, it is made in the shape of a giant palm tree and surrounded by a circular sea wall.

Why is it palm shaped?

The palm tree is important to the history and culture of the Middle East. It is seen as a sign of hospitality—a warm welcome to guests.

HOW MUCH ENERGY DOES THE SUN GIVE US?

In just one hour, Earth receives more energy from the Sun than all humans use in a whole year.

What is a carbon footprint?

The **carbon footprint** of an activity, process, or product is the amount of carbon dioxide it releases.

People in the developed world use far more energy than people in the developing world.

What are fossil fuels?

Fossil fuels are preserved sunshine—when these once-living things burn, they release the energy that they captured from the Sun while alive.

Nearly half of the world's electrical energy is produced by burning fossil fuels such as coal and oil.

What is the carbon footprint of an internet search?

A single search on Google releases around 0.2 g (0.007) of carbon dioxide.

Where is the world's largest hydroelectric plant?

The largest on the planet is China's **Three Gorges Dam**.

The biggest blackout in history happened in India in 2012. The outage left 620 million people without power.

How much energy does the Three Gorges Dam produce?

Its 34 turbines generate the same energy as burning 45 million tonnes (49.6 million tons) of coal.

How does does nuclear fuel compare to fossil fuels?

The nuclear fuel uranium is about 8,000 times more powerful per unit of weight than oil or coal.

CAN STEM CELLS HELP BLIND PEOPLE TO SEE?

What are stem cells?

The human body is made up of some 200 different types of cell. Each of these cell types does a different job. Most cells make exact copies of themselves, but some special cells, called **stem cells**, can morph into almost any type of cell. Doctors harvest these jack-of-all-trade cells and use them to mend damage in the body.

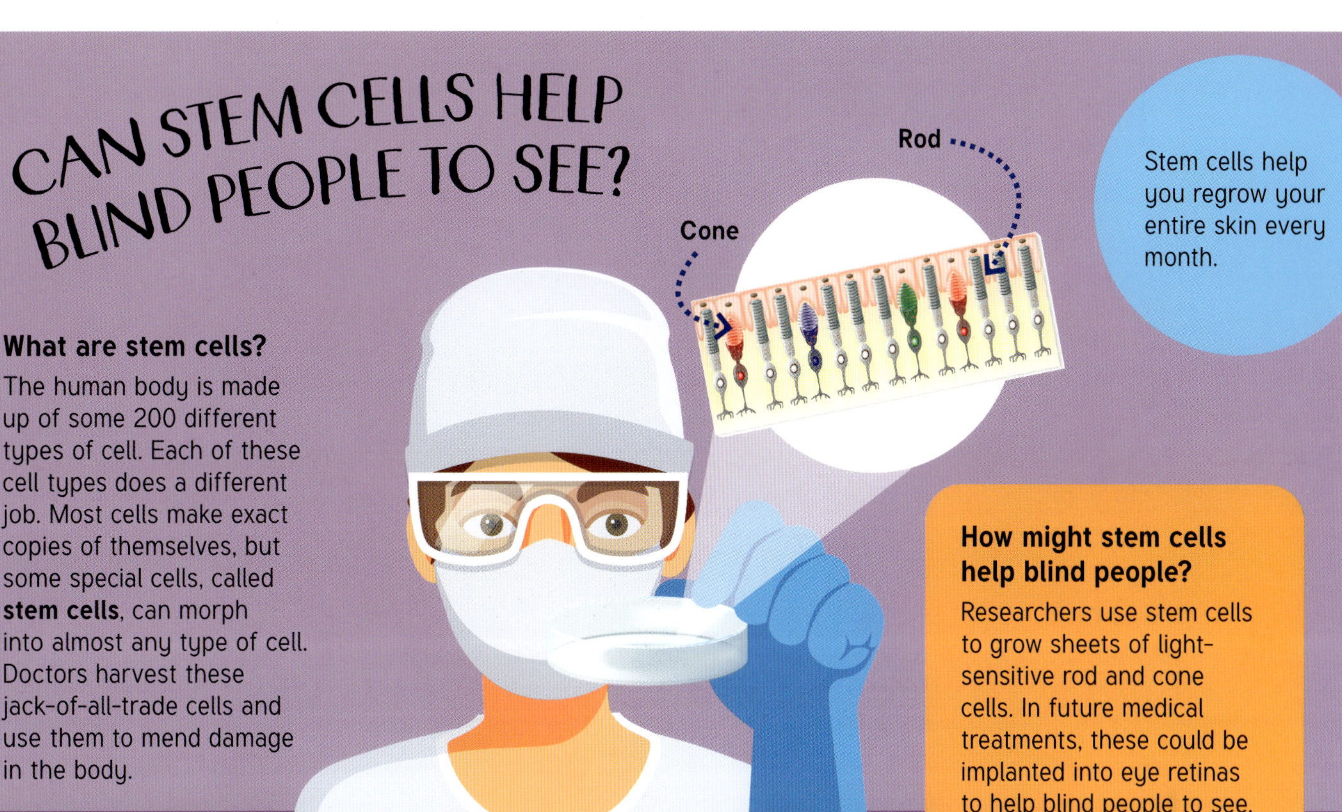

How might stem cells help blind people?

Researchers use stem cells to grow sheets of light-sensitive rod and cone cells. In future medical treatments, these could be implanted into eye retinas to help blind people to see.

CAN NEW HANDS BE PRINTED?

Yes! We can use 3D printing to print a variety of items, including prosthetic hands!

How does 3D printing work?

3D printing builds shapes from the ground up, by laying down layer after layer of melted plastic, squirted out of a tiny nozzle. Slice by horizontal slice, a solid object is built up.

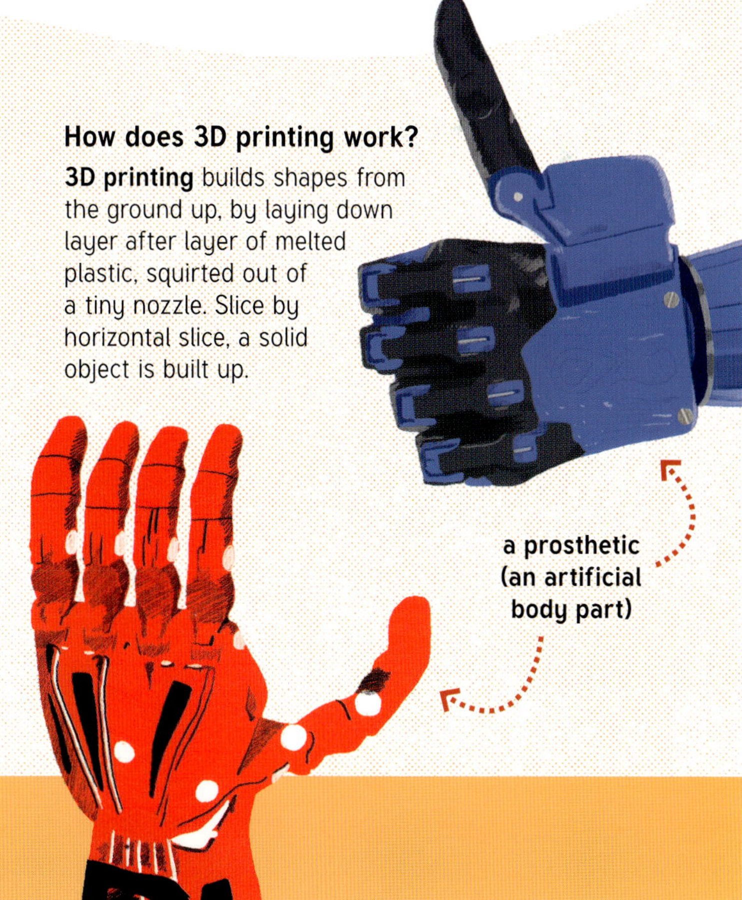

How can you print a new hand?

With a digital file downloaded from the internet, people who have lost a hand, or were born without one, can print out a fully working robotic hand. The 3D-printed plastic hands come in cool, loud shades and look like robot parts. Kids love them and they can get new ones as they grow, because the printed hands are much cheaper than traditional prosthetics.

WHAT WERE THE FIRST CELL PHONES LIKE?

The bulky battery "brick" weighed as much as a bag of sugar, took 10 hours to charge and only had half an hour of talk time.

What was the first phone photo?

Philippe Kahn shared the first picture taken on a phone in 1997. It was a snap of his newborn baby.

When was the first cell phone call made?

The first cell phone call was made on April 3, 1973.

The Nokia 1100 is the top-selling electronic gadget in history, with more than 250 million devices sold.

How much was the first cell phone?

The first cell phones cost around $3,000!

The average smartphone user touches their phone more than 2,600 times a day.

HOW MANY ARTIFICIAL SATELLITES ARE ORBITING EARTH?

Over 11,000 satellites orbit Earth, transmitting telephone and internet communications, and TV and radio signals.

What was the first satellite?

The first artificial satellite was launched on October 4, 1957. Sputnik 1 contained little more than a radio transmitter. The beachball-sized satellite circled the planet for about three months before falling into Earth's atmosphere and burning up.

The Global Positioning System (GPS) uses a fleet of 24 satellites orbiting 24,000 km (11,500 miles) above Earth's surface.

Sputnik 1

Are satellites tracked?

The U.S Space Surveillance Network tracks more than 13,000 items larger than 10 cm (4 in).

WHAT IS THE INTERNET?

The Internet is a vast network of computers around the world, all connected together.

The World Wide Web is the information on the internet—a collection of web pages.

Who invented the internet?

English computer scientist Sir Tim Berners-Lee invented the World Wide Web in 1989.

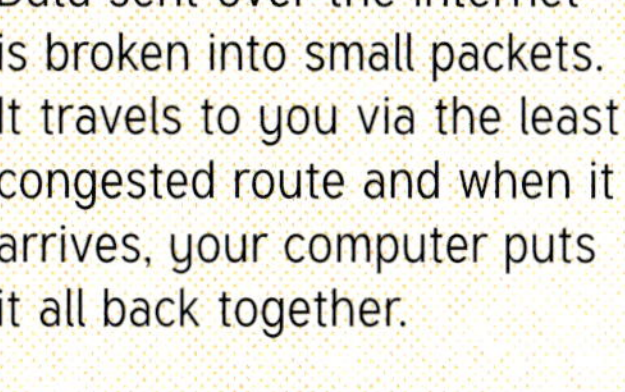

Are sharks a danger to the internet?

Sharks like to chew underwater internet cables.

Data sent over the internet is broken into small packets. It travels to you via the least congested route and when it arrives, your computer puts it all back together.

How many people are online?

The internet connects 5.3 billion people, who access it on 17 billion devices.

About two-thirds of all e-mails are spam.

How heavy is data?

The gazillions of moving electrons that make up the data-in-motion on the internet weigh about the same as one strawberry.

How long are underwater cables?

The longest submarine cable in the world stretches 38,600 km (24,000 miles) and connects 33 countries.

Your online data can be anywhere—individual files can be spread across data centers around the globe.

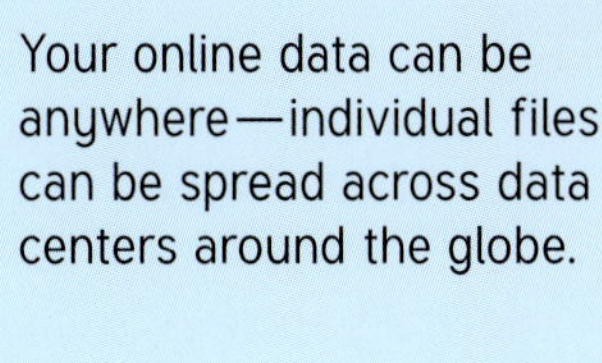

What did the first webcam film?

The world's first webcam was trained on a coffee pot at the computer laboratory at the University of Cambridge, helping people to avoid a wasted trip if the coffee pot was empty.

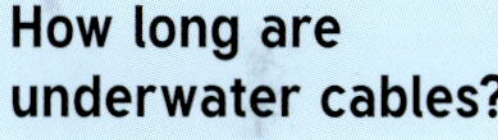

HOW FAST IS THE WORLD'S MOST POWERFUL SUPERCOMPUTER?

The Hewlett Packard Enterprise Frontier has a record-breaking performance measured at 1.206 FLOPS.

Computer speeds are measured in **FLOPS**, which stands for "floating-point operations per second."

Calculation per second = 1 FLOPS

2017 iMac = 1,900,000,000,000 flops (1.9 teraflops)

Sunway TaihuLight = 93,000,000,000,000,000 flops (93 petaflops)

How big are supercomputers?

China leads the world in supercomputers. These titanic machine-brains fill entire warehouses and tackle the biggest problems. They can even calculate the birth and early expansion of the Universe. Supercomputers also try to predict how earthquake waves will travel to find out about the inside of our planet.

WERE THE COMPUTERS ON THE APOLLO SPACECRAFT ONLY AS POWERFUL AS A CALCULATOR?

Yes. An average cell phone today has vastly more power than the computers that took humans to the Moon and back safely.

How much memory did the Apollo computers have?

The computer on board the Apollo spacecraft was more basic than today's toasters. It had just 36 KB of permanent memory—less than many scientific calculators, which have 256 KB.

Did the computer steer the Apollo 11 module?

When Apollo 11's lunar module neared the Moon's surface, the computer overloaded and locked up. Neil Armstrong took the controls and landed the "Eagle" manually with seconds to spare.

Memory match-up
Apollo unit:
6 transistors

iPhone 16: approx.
16 billion transistors

HOW MUCH FASTER ARE QUANTUM COMPUTERS?

Quantum computers are 100 million times faster than your home PC.

Why are quantum computers faster?

Quantum computers use qubits. A **qubit** (say cue-bit) is a "quantum bit." Unlike traditional computer bits, which store information as 0s and 1s, qubits can be set to 0, a 1, or both at the same time! This gives quantum computers a huge boost when it comes to number crunching.

Google's cutting-edge quantum computer is called D-Wave 2X™.

Robots assemble cars—and drive them—disarm bombs, deep-sea dive in Antarctic water, explore distant planets, and vacuum carpets.

WHAT IS THE MEANING OF ROBOT?

Robot comes from a Czech word robota, which means hard work.

How many robots are there?

We may share our planet with 20 million robotic machines by 2030.

What was the first robot?

The first robot ever was a mechanical bird, built in 400 BCE, that flew 200 m (656 ft).

Robots can go into environments that would be dangerous for humans.

HOW MUCH WOULD YOU PAY FOR A PATTY?

The most expensive meat patty cost $331,400.

Why so expensive?

In 2013, two volunteers sat down in front of an audience in London to eat a burger. The strange show was a public tasting of artificially produced beef. The small slab of lab-made meat had taken three months to grow at a cost of $331,400.

How is artificial meat made?

Artificial meat, also known as "schmeat," is made from stem cells taken from a cow's shoulder. In the lab it is grown into long strips of muscles. Fans say that it not only saves animals' lives, but also protects the environment. Critics say it's weird and tastes strange!

HOW MANY GENES ARE NEEDED FOR LIFE?

What are genes?

Genes are short "clips" of DNA held on long coiled strands called **chromosomes**. They contain the coded instructions to keep the body running. Many genes do the same job, however.

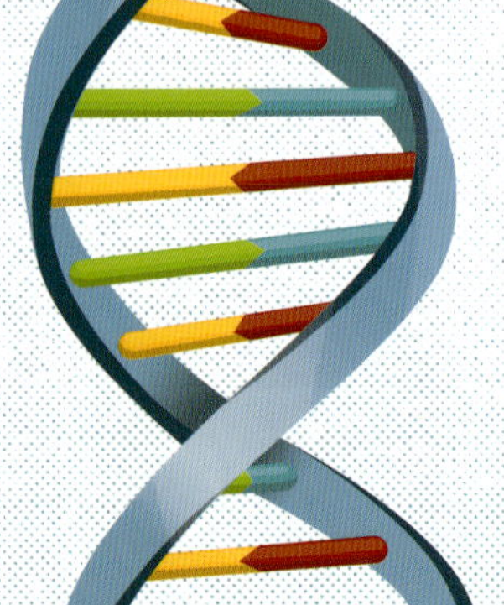

How many genes do bacteria have?

Free-living bacteria normally have around 1,500–7,500 genes.

What is a genome?

A **genome** is the complete set of DNA in a cell.

How many genes are needed for life?

Scientist Craig Venter and his team snipped out genes one by one from a bacterial cell, keeping only the essential ones. They ended up with a fully functioning microbe with just 473 genes—the smallest genome of any single-celled living organism.

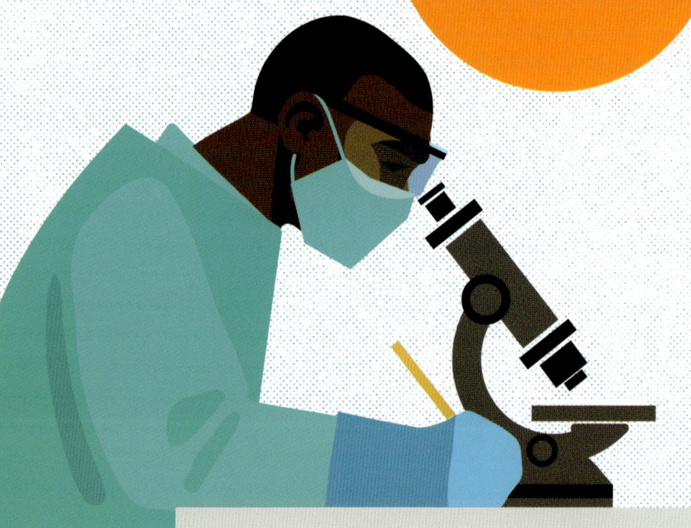

DOES EVERY MAGNET HAVE TWO POLES?

Yes. Although a single magnetic pole—called a monopole—can theoretically exist, no one has detected one yet.

What happens when you divide a magnet?

Split a bar magnet in two, and you don't get separate north and south poles. Instead, you get two new magnets, each with a north and south end—a **dipole**. Even if you go right down to single particles, you still end up with a magnetic dipole.

Is north really south?

Earth's North Pole is actually a south pole. The north pole of a compass magnet is attracted to a magnetic south pole, which is in the geographic North. Confusing!

WHAT IS THE WORLD'S BIGGEST MACHINE?

The **Large Hadron Collider (LHC)** is a ring-shaped particle accelerator that is changing our understanding of the Universe.

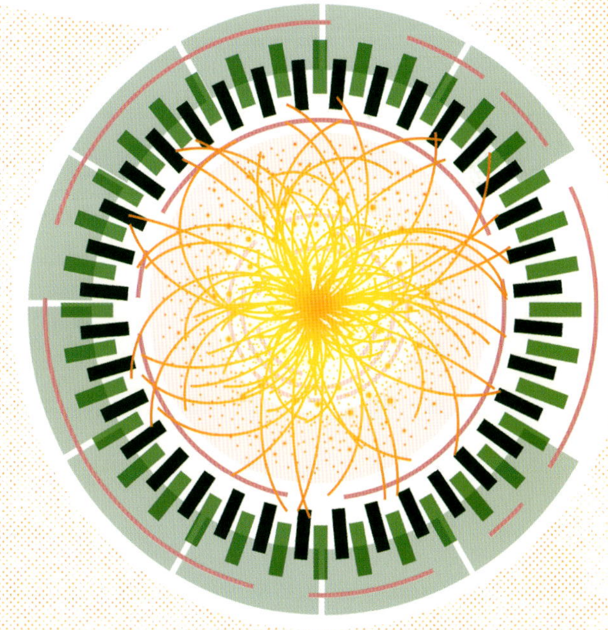

What does the Collider do?

Tiny particles of matter zoom around a tunnel on the French-Swiss border. Protons can do the 27-km (16.7-mile) loop 11,245 times per second—that's very close to the speed of light itself. When they smash together—"BOOM!"—a blinding flash of energy gives us a glimpse of what happened to matter shortly after the Big Bang.

What is the LHC looking for?

After smashing particles together, the LHC searches the "crash site" for unusual types of matter. In 2012, scientists discovered the **Higgs boson particle**, which is thought to give mass to matter.

HOW WEAK IS GRAVITY?

Gravity is the weakest fundamental force.

What does gravity do?

Gravity is the force that keeps our feet on the ground and holds the planets in orbit around the Sun. It certainly doesn't feel weak when you fall down. However, the gravitational pull of the whole planet on an iron nail can be easily beaten by a small bar magnet.

What are the fundamental forces?

Just four interactions keep our Universe ticking. The **strong force** and the **weak force** hold together the nucleus in atoms. **Electromagnetism** has to do with electricity, magnetism, and the way atoms interact. **Gravity** draws objects with mass together.

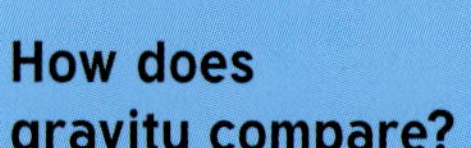
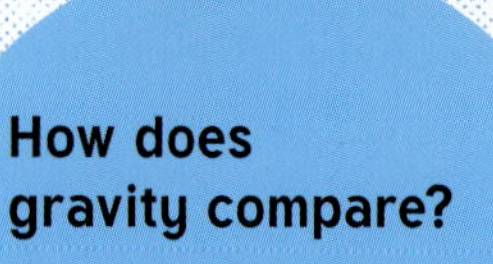

How does gravity compare?

Gravity is 10 thousand trillion trillion trillion times weaker than the electromagnetic force.

ARE ELECTRONS REALLY SLOW?

Electrons in a wire only move at the speed of spreading honey.

If electrons are slow, why do electronic gadgets come on right away?

An electric current is made by electrons moving in a wire. Although individual electrons move sluggishly, the electromagnetic wave that ripples through the wire travels close to the speed of light—around 270,000 km (167,770 miles) per second! This pulse makes all the electrons start moving at almost the same instant.

How slow are electrons?

Electrons in a wire move about 1 mm (0.04 in) per second.

CAN YOU SEE RADIATION?

Our eyes can sense some types of electromagnetic radiation. We call those types **visible light**.

What is microwave radiation used for?
Microwave radiation is used for cell phone networks and to quickly cook food.

Radio waves are mostly used for TV, radio, and telephone communication.

There are other types of electromagnetic radiation that we can't see.

Can radio waves travel into space?
Radio waves can travel around the world and be bounced off satellites in space.

Radio telescopes pick up weak radio waves arriving from outer space.

How do X-rays work?
Penetrating **X-rays** are used to look inside the body, because they travel through muscle, but not bone.

Night-vision goggles

Hot things give off light, too. This infrared radiation is picked up by night-vision goggles.

Are gamma rays dangerous?
Yes. Released by nuclear reactors and bombs, **gamma rays** are the most energetic form of light.

Sizzling **UV rays** from the Sun can cause sunburn.

HOW OLD ARE MICROWAVES?

Microwaves are the earliest light in the Universe. We can't see them though!

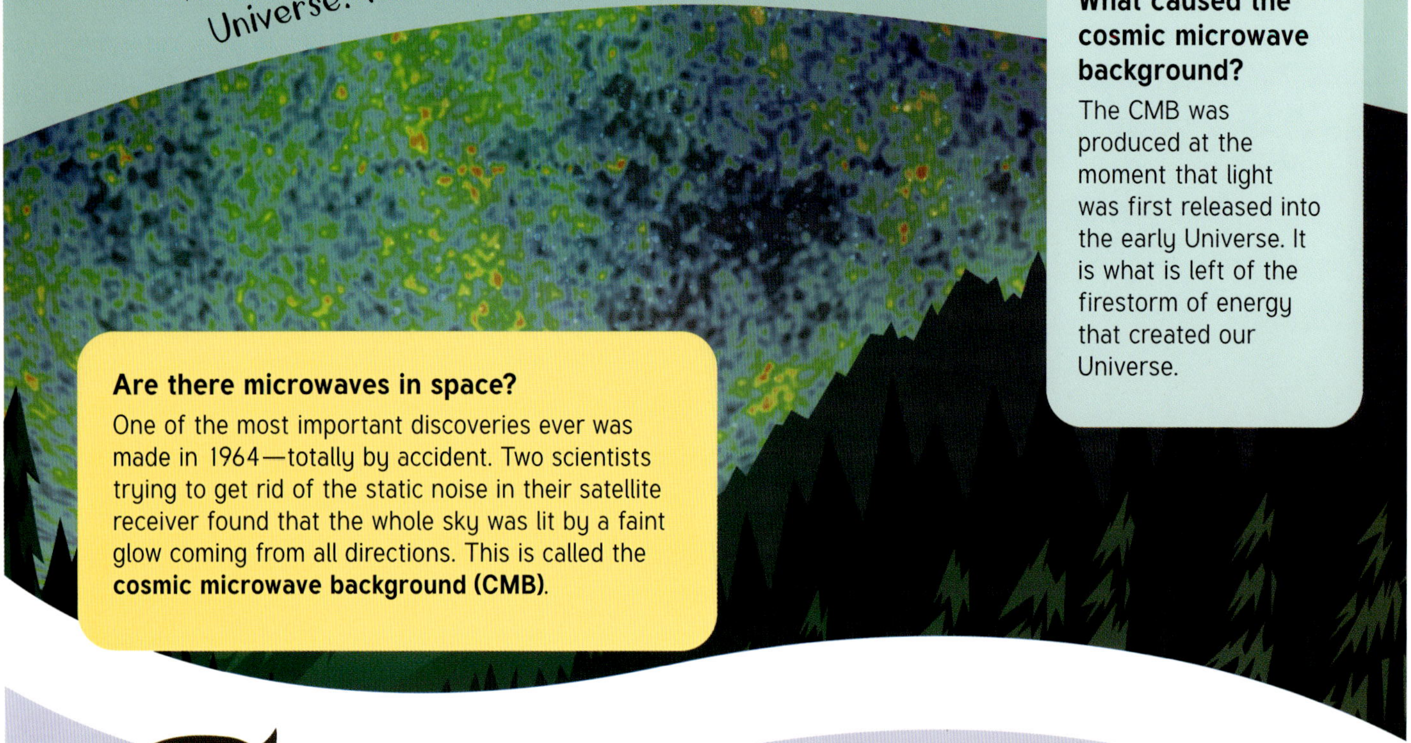

What caused the cosmic microwave background?

The CMB was produced at the moment that light was first released into the early Universe. It is what is left of the firestorm of energy that created our Universe.

Are there microwaves in space?

One of the most important discoveries ever was made in 1964—totally by accident. Two scientists trying to get rid of the static noise in their satellite receiver found that the whole sky was lit by a faint glow coming from all directions. This is called the **cosmic microwave background (CMB)**.

HOW WERE MICROWAVES DISCOVERED?

Useful for defrosting food and making popcorn, the microwave oven is an essential part of a modern kitchen. The appliance was invented in 1946, when engineer Percy Spencer stood next to a magnetron (a microwave-producing tube) and the chocolate bar in his pocket turned into a gooey, sticky mess. Curious, he popped an egg under the device. It exploded, splattering his face with egg.

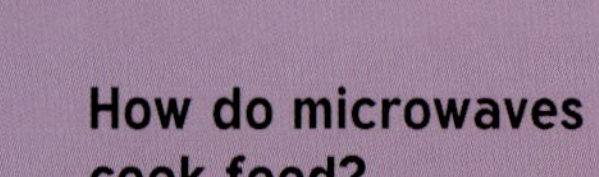

How do microwaves cook food?

Microwaves work by transferring energy to water molecules in the food. As the molecules vibrate more, the food heats up.

Do internet routers send out microwaves?

Yes, but they won't cook you!

WHEN YOU FALL, IS THERE A SPEED LIMIT?

Yes. **Terminal velocity** is the maximum speed at which anything can fall. Jump out of an aircraft and, in theory, you continue picking up speed as you plunge to Earth. In reality, however, the air in the atmosphere resists your movement. At a certain point, air resistance becomes greater than gravity and you slow down, until the forces are balanced. Falling belly down and lying flat like a plank, you can reach a terminal velocity of around 200 km/h (120 mph).

Who fell the fastest?

Daredevil Felix Baumgartner hit 1,357.64 km/h (843.6 mph) during his 2012 skydive from space.

WHAT IS THE LOWEST POSSIBLE TEMPERATURE?

Absolute zero.

How is heat energy measured?

Scientists have a special temperature scale for measuring the heat energy in substances. It is called the **Kelvin scale**, named after the Scottish physicist William Thompson (aka Lord Kelvin). Zero Kelvin is the lower limit of cold, −273.15 °C (-459.67 °F) Called **absolute zero**, it is the temperature at which atoms stop dead and there is no heat energy left.

Can you reach absolute zero?

Absolute zero is actually impossible to reach. That's because no matter how chilly it gets, there is always some energy due to the wiggling of particles at the smallest—quantum—level. This quantum movement is what keeps helium liquid right down to the very coldest temperatures.

IS A PERFECT VACUUM POSSIBLE?

The purest vacuum ever would have no matter in it whatsoever. But even the best vacuum pumps leave the odd particle inside a container. Fingerprint smudges, plastics, and certain metals on the airlocks or walls give off vapor in high-vacuum conditions.

Where is the best vacuum?

The most complete vacuum is in outer space. That is why astronauts wear special pressure suits and carry their own oxygen supply to breathe. However, even space contains tiny particles of cosmic dust floating around, along with atoms of hydrogen and helium.

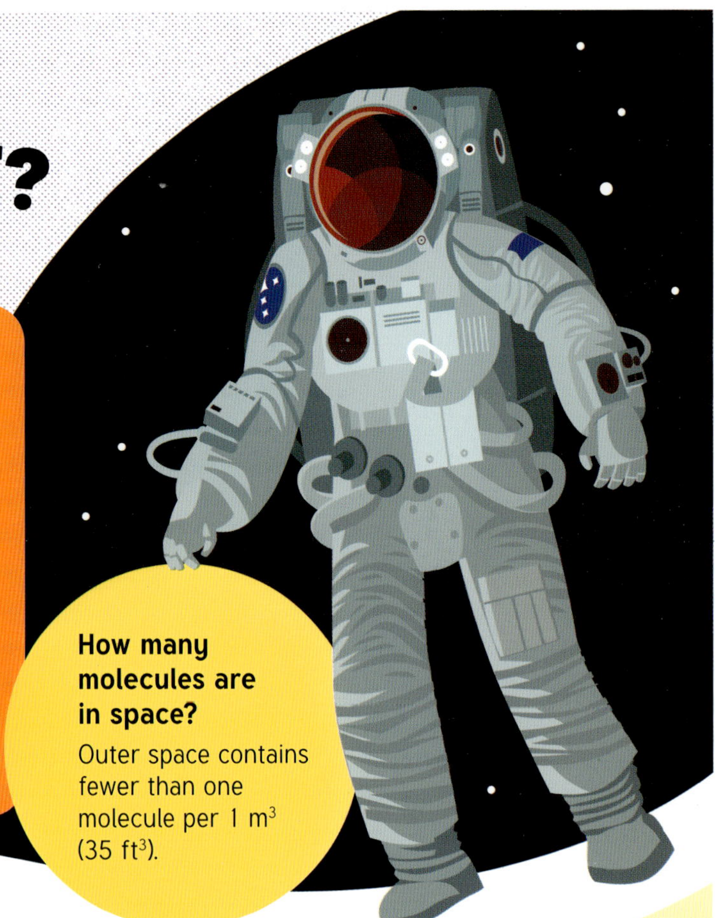

How many molecules are in space?

Outer space contains fewer than one molecule per 1 m³ (35 ft³).

DOES WIND EVER BLOW IN STRAIGHT LINES?

Wind is just the movement of air caused by differences in pressure in the atmosphere. Wind blows from places with a high pressure to lower pressure areas. However, because the planet is spinning, wind travels in curves. This is called the **Coriolis effect**, and it explains why tropical storms swirl clockwise in the northern hemisphere and anticlockwise in the southern hemisphere.

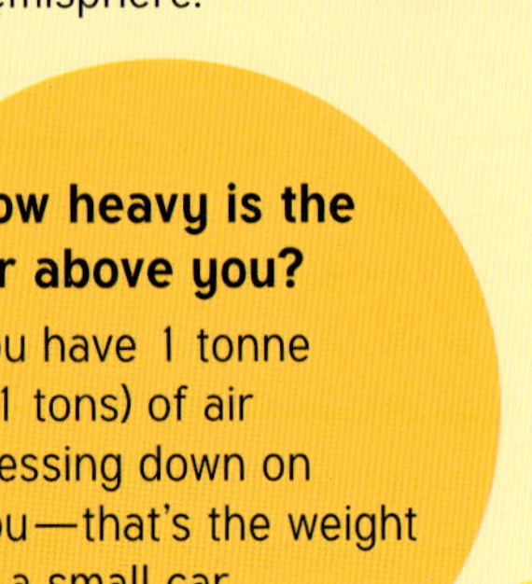

How heavy is the air above you?

You have 1 tonne (1.1 tons) of air pressing down on you—that's the weight of a small car.

WHERE IS THE QUIETEST PLACE ON EARTH?

The quietest place is an echo-free chamber in Minnesota, that absorbs 99.99 percent of sound.

What was the loudest noise?

The loudest sound ever recorded was the eruption of Krakatoa volcano in 1883.

The tremendous crack destroyed the tiny Indonesian island and echoed four times around the planet.

People with "misophonia" hate certain noises such as eating, lip-smacking, pen-clicking, tapping, and typing.

If you could hear it, what would the Sun sound like?

The Sun rings like a bell. Bubbling plasma makes the entire star vibrate.

"Ultrasonic" noises, which humans cannot hear, are used to make pictures of babies in the womb.

Is there a "brown note?"

People sometimes talk about a "brown note"—a sound that makes anyone nearby poop. This is a myth!

What's a good sound to soothe you to sleep?

The sound of rustling leaves or rain on a roof can slow brain activity, and help you get a good night's sleep.

A new fire extinguisher blasts out bass frequencies to put out fires.

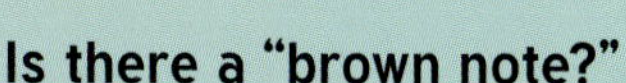

Listening to bass sounds while eating can make your food taste more bitter.

HOW DO PLANES FLY?

What's the secret in the wing shape?

When you climb into a metal tube and zoom off into the sky, it's comforting to know that physics can explain what keeps you up there. Planes' wings are shaped in a way that makes air move faster over the top than underneath the wing. That creates lift.

Lift force

1. Air moving over the top of a wing moves quickly and has low pressure.

2. Air coming off the trailing edge of the wing is thrown down. This also generates an upward force.

3. Higher pressure under the wing generates an upward, lifting force.

DO INVISIBILITY CLOAKS EXIST?

Who hasn't dreamed of slipping unnoticed through crowds of unseeing people?

How would an invisibility cloak work?

Scientists are working with magical-sounding metamaterials. While not yet as good as Harry Potter's invisibility cloak, these divert light rays around them, making it look as if they are not there. Since the light path around an object is longer than one that travels directly through that space, they are still detectable.

How do planes stay out of sight?

Hiding in plain sight usually involves thwarting detection technology. **Stealth planes** have a cunning radar-baffling shape, quiet internal wing-engines, and radar-absorbing paint. However, they still cast shadows.

HOW WERE INVISIBLE ATOMS DISCOVERED?

What gave scientists a clue about atoms?

Stick some smoke particles, dust motes, or pollen grains in water under a microscope and you'll see they do a jittery dance, careering all over the place. Scottish scientist Robert Brown discovered this **Brownian motion** in 1827.

What did Einstein think?

In 1905, über-brain Albert Einstein thought that this random motion might be caused by invisible atoms of gas (or water molecules) colliding with larger smoke or pollen grains. He crunched the numbers and proved mathematically that matter is made of tiny particles, and could even cleverly predict how big atoms are.

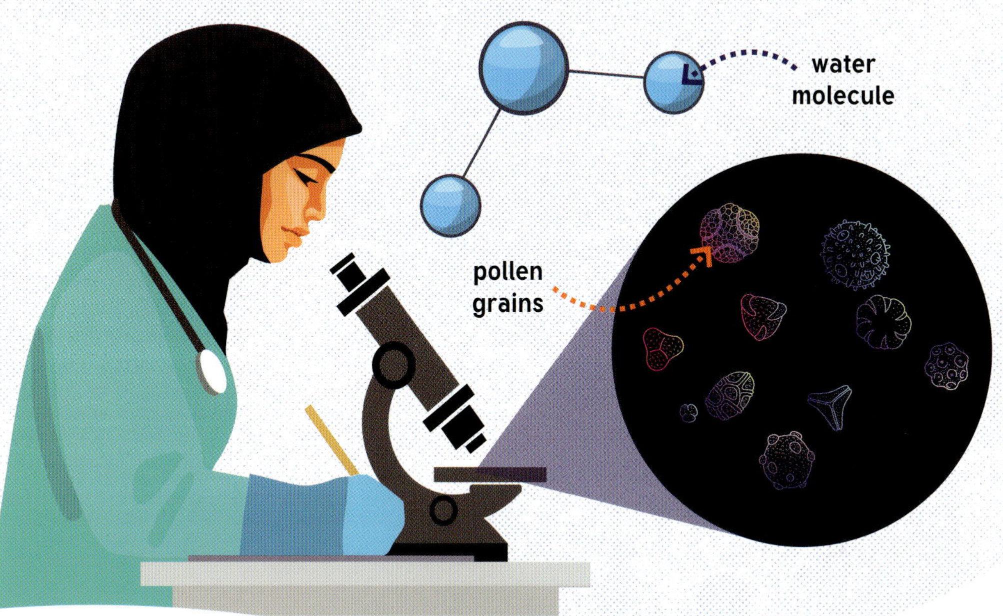

WHO WAS THE FIRST TO SEE MICROBES?

In the 1670s, Antonie van Leeuwenhoek was the first person to gaze upon a hidden world. Leeuwenhoek (say Lay-ven-hook) made the best magnifying glasses in the world, which he used to check the quality of cloth. But when he looked at dirty pond water, he could see wriggling beasts smaller than anything else anyone had ever seen.

Are most living things easy to see?

No, most living things on Earth are tiny single-celled organisms that you need to use a microscope to see.

There are more microbugs in a pinch of soil than there are people on the planet.

WHY DO WE ONLY SEE ONE SIDE OF THE MOON?

Who saw the far side of the Moon first?

The first time humans got to see the "far side" of the Moon was in 1959, thanks to the Soviet spacecraft Luna 3.

Does the Moon always face the same way?

The Moon isn't stuck in place with one side facing us. If it wasn't spinning, we'd see all sides of it as it moves around the planet. Instead, the Moon spins exactly once on its axis every time it orbits Earth, so it always keeps the same side toward us.

This is called **tidal locking**. Earth's larger gravity has acted like a brake and slowed the spin of its smaller companion.

WHERE ARE THE STARS IN THE DAYTIME?

Stars and galaxies don't disappear in the day! They are invisible because the light from our own star is so bright.

What hides the stars?

During the night, we face away from the Sun and the marvels of space are revealed. But as the Earth swings us back around, the radiation streaming off our star makes the sky glow blue and blinds us to the faint light from the stars.

So, why do we see the Moon in the day?

The Moon is bright enough to be visible in the daytime. Unless there is a new moon, you can see it nearly every day.

IS LIGHT A PARTICLE OR A WAVE?

Amazingly, it is both!

How is light like a wave?

Visible light is the type of electromagnetic radiation that humans can see. It ripples through electric and magnetic fields and, unlike a sound wave or a wave moving through water, it doesn't need "stuff" to travel through. Because it can cross the empty vacuum of space, we can see light from the stars.

Light, moving as a ripple

How is light like a particle?

Other experiments show that light comes in packages or blips called **photons**. Photons fly through space like tiny bullets.

WHAT'S WEIRD ABOUT THE QUANTUM WORLD?

At the smallest scale, the rules are very different.

Does the quantum world follow rules?

Scientists exploring the world at a quantum scale—smaller even than atoms—have found a place with very different rules. Quantum particles can only have fixed amounts of energy, and "click" between them with no in-between amounts, a bit like gears on a bike. In the normal-sized world, however, you don't notice the tiny quantum effects.

What is quantum energy?

When light interacts with subatomic particles, it is "chunked." Each packet of light—or photon—carries a fixed amount of energy.

Photons

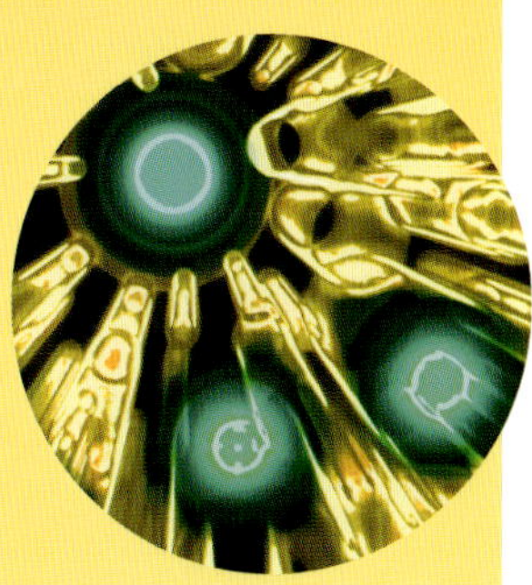

HOW CAN A PARTICLE BE IN TWO PLACES?

The rules of the Universe are very different in the quantum realm!

One of the spookiest quantum effects is that particles can be in two places at the same time.

It's impossible to know where a particle is and know its speed at the same time.

Are particles in pairs?

Particles can get paired with each other, so that what happens to one will affect the other.

How far apart can these paired particles be?

This "quantum entanglement" works even if the particles are at opposite ends of the Universe.

What is quantum tunneling?

Quantum tunneling is where particles appear on the other side of a barrier, without moving over or through it.

How is this useful?

Quantum tunneling is how the microchip switches in electronic devices work.

Is teleportation possible?

In 2017, Chinese scientists used quantum entanglement to teleport photons from the surface of Earth into space.

Can we see quantum effects in action?

Quantum effects keep life on Earth going—without them, the Sun would stop shining and plants would not be able to take energy from sunlight.

European robins have a magnetic sense. Experiments have shown that these use quantum effects!

ARE THERE PARALLEL UNIVERSES?

There may be* many yous in many alternate Universes.

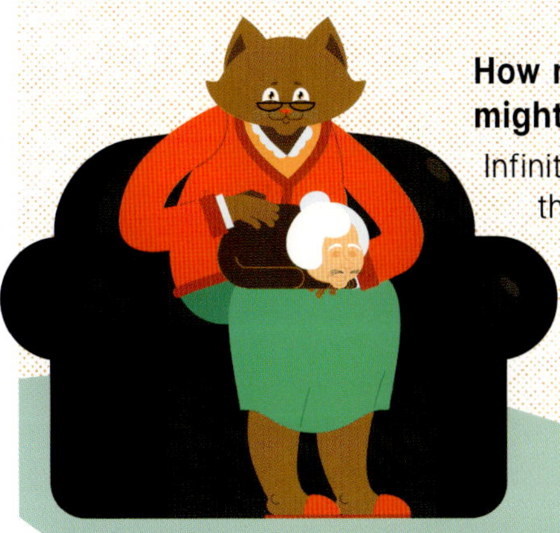

How many might there be?

Infinitely many. If the theories are true,** there could be countless other worlds.

Is this a multiverse?

"Uni" means one. Our Universe is one, single, exapnding universe. As yet, there is no concrete evidence to suggest we are living in a multiverse.

How can there be many "me"s?

Because if there are infinite worlds, there are countless Earths and countless "you"s. Every conceivable possibility happens—in one you're at the top of the heap, in the other, you're at the very bottom.

*In theory!
**We have no way of proving this ... yet!

WHAT CAUSES THE UNIVERSE'S BIGGEST EXPLOSIONS?

Satellites launched in the 1960s made an unexpected discovery— gamma-ray bursts.

What are gamma-ray bursts?

Gamma-ray bursts (GRBs) are flashes of ultra-high energy radiation coming from outer space. Lasting as little as a few milliseconds, they capture the moment a massive star dies. They are the brightest and most powerful bangs in the Universe.

Are they rare?

Scientists have found about 6,000 GRBs to date. About two flash in the sky every day. Luckily for us on Earth, our atmosphere mops up dangerous gamma rays.

How bright are they?

GRBs shine a million times brighter than an entire galaxy!

WHAT IS THE UNIVERSE'S TOP SPEED?

The speed of light.

DO NOT EXCEED

299,792 KM PER SECOND

(186,282 MILES PER SECOND)

If things could travel faster, reality would be in trouble—an arrow might hit its target before a bow was fired!

What does E = mc² mean?

The most famous equation in science says that mass and energy are the same thing. Since light has no mass, it zips along at max speed. Particles of matter, however, need energy to make them go faster, and so gain extra mass. This means they need more and more energy until finally, there isn't enough energy in the Universe to push them to the speed of light.

Can you see a black hole?

No light comes out of a black hole, so it can't be seen. Black holes have so much matter squeezed inside them, they have incredibly strong gravity.

How do you avoid being sucked in?

To escape Earth's gravitational pull, an object must travel 11 k/s (6.8 miles/sec)— about 33 times the speed of sound. That's an engineering problem. But the escape velocity from a black hole's gravity is greater than the speed of light. That's physically impossible for anything in our Universe.

What would happen if you fell into a black hole?

Its super-strong gravity would stretch you into spaghetti in an instant!

WHAT MYSTERY SUBSTANCE IS PULLING THE UNIVERSE APART?

Dark energy is the single biggest unsolved problem in science.

How much dark energy is there?

Calculating the energy that is needed to defeat gravity, we find that dark energy must make up 70 percent of everything. It's hard to believe, but we are completely in the dark about three-quarters of our Universe!

Is our Universe getting bigger or smaller?

Our Universe is getting bigger. Instead of being slowed by the gravity of all the billions and trillions of stars it contains, its expansion is speeding up! Some mystery energy is defeating the force of gravity and astronomers can't explain it. That is why they call it "dark" energy.

How big is the universe?

Unimaginably big, that's all you really need to know!

How much can we see of it?

The part that we can see today extends about 14 billion light years in every direction. That forms an unimaginably massive sphere 28 billion light years across. But that is not all there is.

CAN WE SEE ALL OF THE UNIVERSE?

Observatory

What's missing?

We can only see as far as light has journeyed over the Universe's lifetime. Space has expanded faster, however, whisking lots of the cosmos away and out of view.

How big might the Universe be?

Estimates vary, but the Universe might be 250 times bigger than what we can observe.

MIGHT AN ASTEROID END THE WORLD?

The Planetary Defense Coordination Office (PDCO) in Washington D.C., USA, keeps the world safe from impacts from outer space.

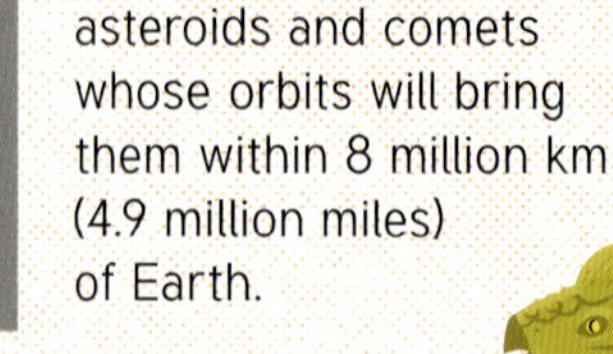

Are there many large asteroids?

There are 1,489 potentially hazardous asteroids, bigger than 100 m (328 ft) across, that may come very close to Earth.

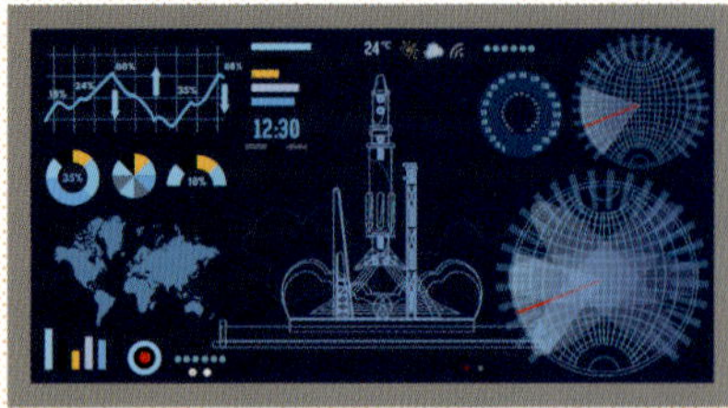

The PDCO monitors asteroids and comets whose orbits will bring them within 8 million km (4.9 million miles) of Earth.

When was the last big impact?

About 65 million years ago. It killed off the non-avian dinosaurs.

How common are impacts?

An asteroid up to 10 km (6.2 miles) wide smashes into Earth about once every 100 million years.

How else might the world end?

A gamma-ray burst from a nearby star could fry our planet with radiation.

1. In about 5 billion years, our own star will start to die …

2. The Sun will become a red giant. Its outer surface will balloon outward and swallow up the inner planets.

3. Earth's surface will be scorched, turning it as lifeless as that of Venus.

Should you worry?

It's true … one day, Planet Earth will be no more. However, humans might be living on other planets by then.

Could the Universe be eaten up?

Some scientists believe that black holes will eat up everything else in the Universe.

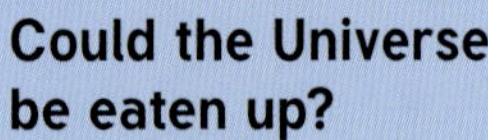

IN 1977, WERE WE CONTACTED BY ALIENS?

What was heard?

It's 10:15 pm on August 15, 1977. Jerry Ehman is manning the Big Ear radio telescope in Delaware, Ohio. Suddenly, the equipment crackles with a pulse of radio waves coming out of the constellation of Sagittarius. It is 30 times more powerful than the background noise. Excitedly, he scribbles "Wow!" across the computer printout.

Did we reply?

The 72-second "Wow!" signal has never happened again, and some people are SURE that this was contact with real-life aliens. In 2012, the Arecibo radio telescope in Puerto Rico beamed back a reply. The big "Hello from Earth" contained 10,000 Twitter messages, plus videos from celebrities.

Big Ear radio telescope

COULD THERE BE 40 BILLION PLANETS SIMILAR TO EARTH ORBITING DISTANT SUNS?

How many have been spotted?

Kepler has spotted over 2,700 exoplanets.

Where should we look?

There are countless places that life might be hiding in the galaxy, but it makes sense to look for other planets like Earth. Because scientists think that liquid water is essential for life, they concentrate their search on "Goldilocks" planets—those planets that are "not too hot, not too cold, but just right," for water.

How do you find them?

NASA's Kepler space probe stares at distant stars, trying to spot a planet. It looks for shadows cast by planets as they cross the face of the star. Wobbles in starlight also help to detect invisible planets.

Too hot!

Too cold!

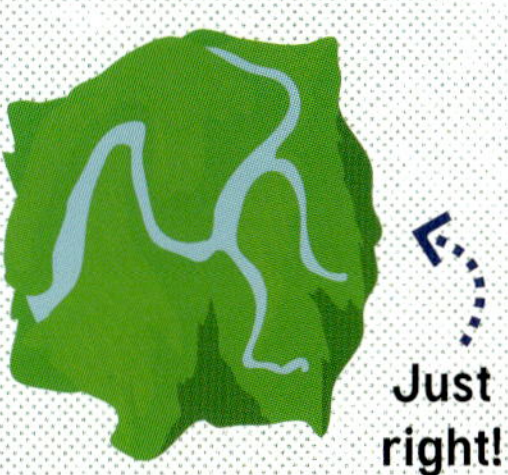

Just right!

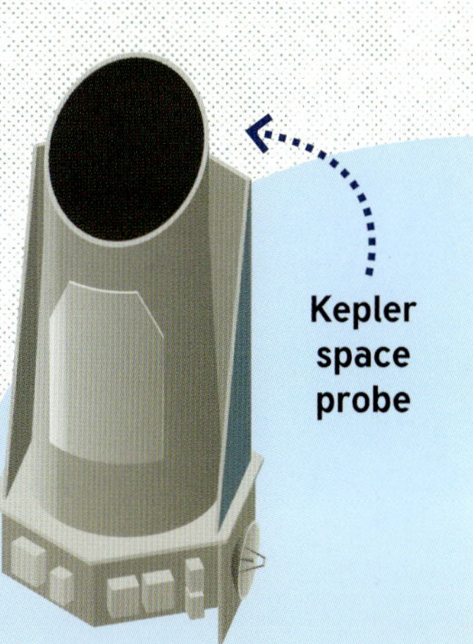

Kepler space probe

WHAT GIVES CRYSTALS THEIR SHAPES?

How big can crystals grow?
The world's largest crystals are 11 m (36 ft) long—that's the same as 58 pencils laid end-to-end.

Do atoms shape crystals?

Crystals are beautiful natural solids. The atoms inside a crystal are invisible. They may not show how they are organized, but they leave some pretty big hints on the surface. Their flat faces, sharp edges, and angles all reflect their orderly internal arrangement.

How can we see the atoms in crystals?

To see the invisible internal arrangements of atoms, we fire invisible X-rays at them. These rays bounce off the atoms and the reflections reveal their hidden structure.

ARE VIRUSES SMALLER THAN BACTERIA?

Yes! Viruses are the smallest living things.

How do viruses spread?

Viruses are out for themselves. They spread by hijacking living cells and turning them into zombie virus factories. The cell ignores warning signals and keeps pumping out copies of the invader. This ends badly for the cell. Ripped open, it dies, releasing many new viruses to infect other cells. Fighting viral infections is what makes people feel ill. The common cold, flu, chicken pox, and measles are all illnesses caused by viruses.

The body does have ways of fighting back against viruses.

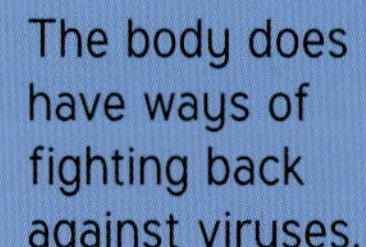

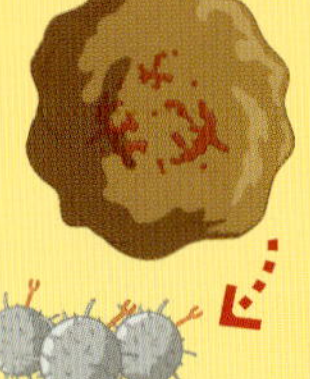

1. One type of white blood cell surrounds viruses.

2. It engulfs them and breaks them down.

3. Other white blood cells make antibodies.

4. Antibodies are designed to detect specific viruses.

5. Once they find the viruses, they destroy them.

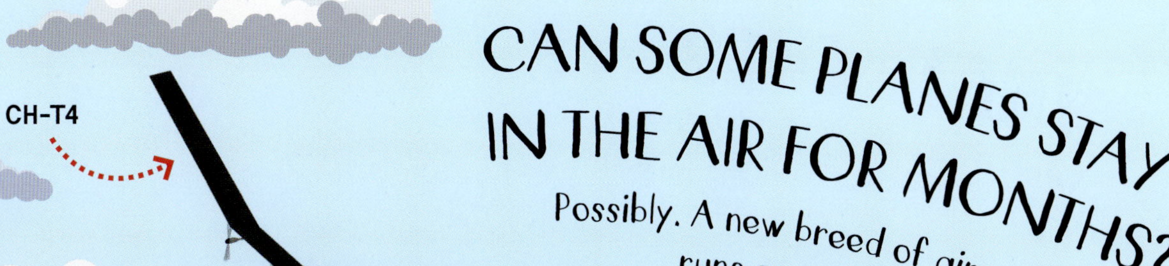

CAN SOME PLANES STAY IN THE AIR FOR MONTHS?

Possibly. A new breed of aircraft runs on sunshine.

Do solar-powered planes need pilots?

The Chinese solar-powered drone, **CH-T4**, is huge, but doesn't need a pilot. Designed as a giant flying wing, it cruises 20 km (12 miles) above the ground. Its 40- m (131- ft) wings are as long as three long-distance buses, but the CH-T4 weighs just 400 kg (880 lbs). This lightweight drone is powered by sunshine, so it doesn't need to refuel.

How far can solar-powered planes fly?

In 2016, **Solar Impulse 2** became the first solar-powered plane to complete a full circuit of the planet.

WHAT IS THE WORLD'S SMELLIEST CHEMICAL?

Thioacetone is a substance so stinky it makes people pass out.

What happens if you sniff it?

In 1889, in Freiberg, Germany, a factory attempted to produce **thioacetone**. It caused mass panic! People were fainting and being sick all over the place. They tried to flee town to escape its foul smell.

What else tops the stinky chart?

Two other contenders in the stench stakes are:

- **Skatole**—the smell of poop.
- **Mercaptan**, which is added to natural gas to alert people to gas leaks. It smells of rotting cabbages and smelly socks.

Just one drop of thioacetone is enough to create a whiff nearly 500 m (1,650 ft) away!

WHAT IS ENERGY?

You cannot see energy.
You cannot hold it. So ...

Energy is the stuff that makes things happen. You can observe its effects—food gives people energy. The faster the moving thing, the bigger the smash. Energy doesn't exist on its own; instead, it is always carried by something.

One of the most basic laws of physics is that energy can't be created or destroyed.

Energy is nothing more than a (very) useful idea. This one:

Energy is the ability to do work.*

*Work means moving something against a force.

WHY DOES YOUR BEDROOM END UP A MESS?

What happens to energy in the end?

The Universe is only here because of energy. It can't be created or destroyed ... but what happens to it over time? The answer is **entropy**.

What is entropy?

There are loads of different kinds of energy, and it happily swaps from one kind to another. However, you can't stop energy spreading out. This is why coffee gets cold and why smells spread.

Is a mess more likely?

The same spreading out thing happens with your bedroom. Because there are many more ways in which your room can be messy than tidy, messy is much more likely. Explain that to your folks—"it's not me, it's entropy!"

WHAT IS "HOT ICE" AND "COLD BOILING WATER?"

British climbers complain they can't make a decent cup of tea in high mountains. This is because at lower pressures, water boils at lower temperatures. And tea made in less-than-boiling water does not make a tasty drink. In space, where there is no air pressure, water boils instantly (and then the water vapor freezes instantly).

How do you make ice hotter than boiling water?

The "Z-machine" in New Mexico can create super-high pressures, about 120,000 times above normal air pressure. Water squeezed so tightly forms ice that is hotter than the boiling point of water.

On the summit of the highest mountains, water boils at 72 °C (161 °F).

HOW LONG DO PLASTIC BAGS LAST?

Your plastic trash will still be hanging around in the year 2500.

Can plastic be composted?

Microorganisms can't break down plastic products, but plastic bags and bottles do decompose in sunlight. UV rays break chemical bonds, and the plastic slowly breaks into smaller and smaller pieces.

An estimated 1 trillion plastic bags are thrown away every year.

Does plastic end up in the sea?

Plastic discarded into the Pacific is carried on ocean currents to The Great Pacific Garbage Patch, an area as big as Texas. The plastic is broken down into tiny micro-plastic shards and swirls in great, murky clouds, releasing toxins into the water that pose a danger to sea creatures.

CAN PEOPLE SEE WHAT YOU'RE THINKING?

No, scientists are only just beginning to reveal the mysteries of the brain.

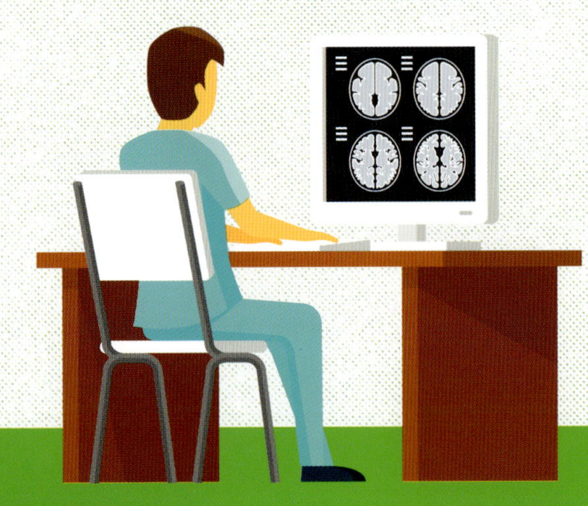

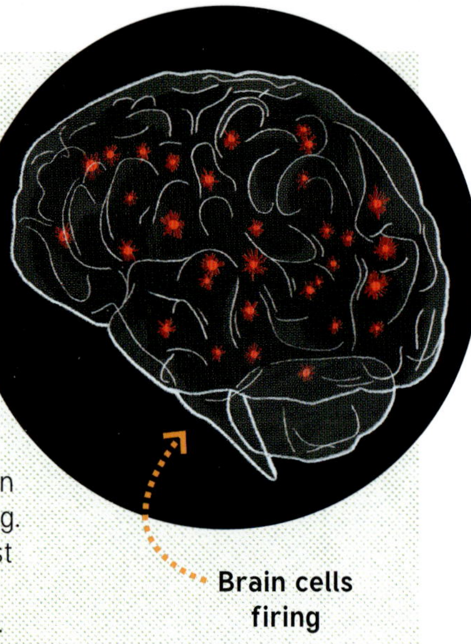

Brain cells firing

How do you read a mind?

For most of history, scientists could only look at the brains of dead people (or use damaged brains to figure out which parts did what). Now, thanks to CT and MRI scans, they can watch a living brain thinking. However, not even our most advanced machines can show us our own thoughts. MRI machines can, however, trace brain activity. We can watch the amazing sight of individual brain cells firing, but we can't read each other's minds.

The human brain is the most complex known structure in the Universe.

IS THE AIR POISONING US?

Invisible toxic particles in the air are poisoning our cities.

How can we reduce the pollution?

Some cities are banning diesel vehicles because they cause more pollution than other types of vehicles.

What type of pollution is in the air?

Nitrogen dioxide is a brown gas. This waste product of burning fossil fuels causes breathing difficulties.

Where is the pollution coming from?

Air pollution is made of poisonous gases, and fine, almost-invisible particles of soot, dust, and chemicals. These come from the exhaust gases of road traffic, power stations, factories, fires, and chemical and paint spraying. Breathing them in is harmful to the lungs over a long period, particularly for children.

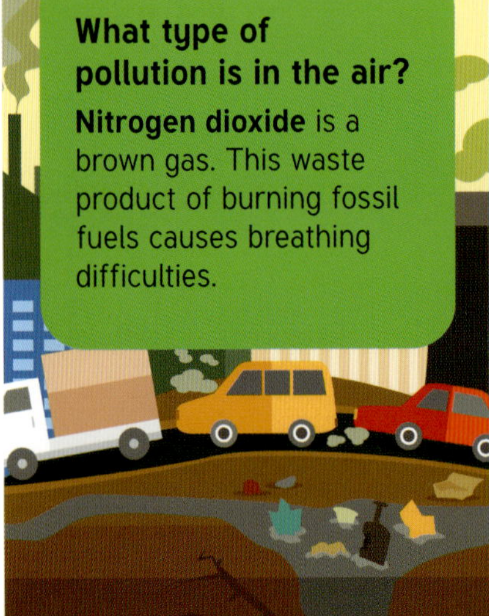